The Reviewers Pr
the First Edition of "Mr. Right

It makes the reader think in an incredibly new light about all sorts of topics…A book of clean, crisp writing that could be read in an hour, but should be savored for a few minutes at a time, and thought about for hours. The world needs more counsellors and priests and politicians with the insight and compassion of Gregory Flood.

—Hugh Shaber, *Lambda Rising Book Report*

Although directed primarily at Gay men [this] is a book that everyone in the world should read!…Gregory Flood *is* Mr. Right!

—*The Works*

Flood spares us crocodile tears and capricious speculation; he offers instead pragmatic possibilities.

—*HALO Magazine*

His sentiments, marvelously free of sentimentality, are lucid and life-affirming, the personal projected clearly on to the universal.

—*In Touch for Men*

He dares us to stop repeating the pat phrases that we hear every Sunday over brunch and start viewing our lives as gay men from a slightly different angle.

—Larry Picard, *GFNB Newsletter*

Flood's book contains ideas which are controversial and indispensable at the same time, and which must be considered important to forming a well-rounded attitude about the AIDS experience.

—*City Heights Cable Show*

The Readers Praise Gregory Flood

Bravo! You've said what has needed to be said for years! — *M.D., Atlanta*

Your humor, intelligence and clarity of thought, as well as the joy with which you present your ideas made reading your book an absolute pleasure.—*L.P., New York*

After your seminar . . . I looked myself in the mirror and said, "You're going to be all right." — *D.F., New York*

You are absolutely right on. You are lovingly confrontive. You are outrageous and current, courageous and caring. You know what real life is all about. You tickled my funny bone and impressed my intellect.— *H.S., Honolulu*

[This book] will be given to many of my clients who are still not able to accept themselves as okay. —*R.R., Los Angeles*

The book can benefit our national community tremendously.
                                                    — *M.B., Milwaukee*

The fact that your healing work combines humor as well as love is an inspiration to my mind and is deeply moving for me personally.
                                                    —*A.M., Sacramento*

I'm Looking for Mr. Right, But I'll Settle for Mr. Right Away

**AIDS, True Love, the Perils of Safe Sex
and Other Spiritual Concerns of the Gay male**

Gregory Flood

*Gay 90s Edition
Revised and Expanded*

First Edition © 1986
Gay 90s Edition © 1994

Published by Brob House Books

Letters to the author may be addressed to:
Greg Flood
c/o Brob House Books
1202 E. Pike, #1090
Seattle WA 98122

Original Version:
First printing 1986
Second printing 1987
Gay 90s Edition:
First printing 1994

Cover and page design by Fyodor Roggel

Cover photo by Tom Mapel

Printed in the United States

Dedication
to the Gay 90s Edition

To Pam Peniston again

When everybody else went to find another party,
you stayed.

Acknowledgments

Special thanks to Connie Butler, Karen Wolfson (aka Sister Perfect), Tom Ellicott, Bill-Bailey Carter, Ken Bahm and Chris Smith for their input on this book while it was still in manuscript form. And special thanks to James "Sonny" Alderman.

As I grow older and older,
And totter towards the tomb,
I find that I care less and less
Who goes to bed with whom.

—*Dorothy Sayers*

About the Author

Gregory Flood made his way through a wide variety of spiritual teachings over the years, trying to find one that didn't insult his intelligence. Raised in the Roman Catholic church he went on to Bible studies, Hinduism, Buddhism, the Tarot and psychic phenomenon; he studied Transcendental Meditation with Maharishi Mahesh Yogi and went on to become a TM-Siddha. He eventually abandoned all these approaches to Truth.

After a refreshing period of atheism, Greg was dragged, kicking and screaming, to his first New Thought Sunday service. He realized at once—however grudgingly—that he had found what he'd been looking for. He later took his practitioner training with Religious Science International and served as a licensed Religious Science practitioner, devoting most of his attention and energies to the healing of AIDS.

After publication of his book, Greg presented his dynamic and thought-provoking seminars in major cities nationwide, and for three years served as the director of the Spiritual Science Foundation in Seattle, Washington.

"We are thinking, learning beings," says Greg, "and our beliefs must make sense to us if we are to live profitably with them. The usual method of teaching spirituality—namely, 'This only makes sense if you don't try to make sense out of it'—is ridiculous. Our intelligence is part of our basic equipment. It is not enough for us to believe. We must know. Believing something in my heart, believing it with every fiber of my being, believing it beyond a shadow of a doubt has never saved me from being dead wrong."

Contents

*This is a radically expanded and revised version of **I'm Looking for Mr. Right, But I'll Settle for Mr. Right Away**. Every chapter contains large amounts of new material and several chapters were written in their entirety for this edition.*

(continued ➡)

Sorta True Stories

Mindwork

Affirmations

Appendices

Introduction

Wickedness is a myth invented by good people to
account for the curious attractiveness of others.
—*Oscar Wilde*

There's a T-shirt on the market that says "So Many Men, So
Little Sex."

Ain't it the truth?

I know that shirt is selling well because I see it on so
many chests, the letters riding across the inevitably perfect
pectorals (the rest of the body may look like hell, but the pecs
are always porno star perfect).

It's illuminating that so many gay men complain about
their lack of sexual fulfillment when we're supposed to be
the most promiscuous people on earth. Our social lives
revolve around pickup bars, and yet so many of us never
manage to pick up much of anything besides...well, you
finish that sentence for yourself.

The AIDS epidemic gets blamed for a lot of this. Lonely
gay men complain that the fear of disease makes it very
difficult to meet people, unlike the free-and-easy promiscuous atmosphere of the 1970s. I often suspect—in fact, I'm
sure—that most of these same guys were just as hard up in
1975 as they are today. In the 70s we complained that it was
difficult to establish a relationship because of all the casual
sex that was available in gay life; now that everybody has
supposedly toned down their sexual activity in the wake of
AIDS, we're saying *that's* why it's hard to find a man.
Meanwhile, gay magazines publish articles on how fear of
AIDS is encouraging gay men to settle down in monoga-

mous relationships. It makes you wonder if anybody out there knows what the hell he's talking about.

True love is, of course, rarer than iced tea in the Sahara.

That we're scorned as sex maniacs by the bulk of society while achieving little sexual gratification in our daily lives is more irony than I care to deal with.

Why are we missing the boat?

———

Gays and straights have this in common: we've all been taught to hate homosexuality. The fact that some of us grew up to be what we were taught to despise doesn't exempt us from the effects of this conditioning.

I believe that we gay men—except for the occasional rare fellow—are trudging through life under a crippling weight of lousy ideas about ourselves. I believe that these negative ideas are the causes of our lovelessness, our health crises, our financial messes, our career frustrations, and whatever other goddamnedness we find ourselves saddled with. We're unaware of these ideas, but they're there inside us, working away. We would never *consciously* think such awful things about ourselves, but the mind contains many surprises.

This is a book about those ideas: what they are, how we came to be functioning with them unknowingly, and, most important, how we can clean them out of our heads forever.

We'll be using the term "consciousness" a great deal. And it seems whenever "consciousness" pops up anywhere, somebody wants a definition of it.

The definition of "consciousness" is simple: *consciousness* is a word.

What does the word mean? You already know. So do I. So do all your friends; just ask them.

It's not my purpose to get everybody on earth to agree with the ideas in this book. I've never read a book whose every idea I could agree with, so I certainly don't expect to have written one. Neither is it my purpose to sell you some theological bill of goods. Gay people have suffered miserable treatment at the hands of organized religion, and I understand entirely if your hackles rise at the mere mention of the word "God."

There's nothing wrong with the word "God." It is, in fact, just another word. But it's a word that, in most people's minds, is freighted with so much superstition, guilt, and anger that it's virtually unusable in our discussion here.

The purpose of this book is simply to give you some new ideas about yourself.

Maybe it already has.

Enjoy.

Atlanta 1986⬆

⬇Seattle 1994

"The purpose of this book is simply to give you some new ideas about yourself."

Oh, please, girl friend.

I should have written something like, "The purpose of this book is to challenge your assumptions about absolutely everything."

Hindsight.

The first edition of **I'm Looking for Mr. Right** came before the public in December of 1986. I've spent the ensuing seven years listening to people tell me what the book is about. Some of their interpretations have been, well, extraordinary.

The book's treatment in the gay press has been in general extremely favorable, though not uniformly so. I've been hailed as the gay Gandhi (thanks, but no thanks) and denounced as the Prince of Politically Incorrect Darkness. An editorial cartoon in a recent newsletter of a prestigious AIDS support organization referred to me as "an opportunistic infection" (along with Louise Hay and one other). One day I received in the mail two press clippings from gay publications, one praising me as a safe sex advocate, the other condemning me for telling people not to bother with safe sex. (Neither reviewer understood what I was saying on the subject.)

But whatever their eminencies in the gay establishment had to say about the book, the gay reading public scarfed up all the copies of it faster than they could be printed.

It's all been very exciting. The book inspired gay event organizers to invite me to give seminars, a strange turn of events that found me piled breathlessly into a variety of planes, trains and automobiles that carried me to just about any major city I've ever wanted to go to in order to speak to crowds of gay strangers who, stranger yet, seemed vitally interested in what I had to say.

I've facilitated two wonderful AIDS healing circles and so was given the chance to witness firsthand the spectacular healing capacities of ordinary people. I established my own teaching organization, called the Spiritual Science Foundation, and after a few years, closed it down. I've taught evening classes, preached my own sarcastic kind of sermons and watched sullen, intellectual gay men transform themselves into happy, balanced, fulfilled human beings.

And boy, are my arms tired.

The volume you hold in your hands is a radically expanded version of the original book. As a matter of fact, Chapter Eight—which is entirely new material appearing here for the first time—by itself is as large as the entire text of the first edition. After seven years, I found I had a few more things to say.

However, the original book is still here almost in its entirety, with a few dated references edited out and a few pieces of pretentious vocabulary changed (for instance, in my teaching I no longer refer to the "subconscious mind," a psychological term which I now feel is overused—and often misused—by spiritual teachers).

This new, "Gay Nineties" version is also presented in response to the many gay men who've approached me at speaking engagements over the years and said, "I agree with your ideas; but now what do I do about it?" The original incarnation of the book was a little short on technique, a shortcoming that the present edition makes up for. (It contains a total of ten Mindwork assignments, nine affirmations, and nine "Sorta True Stories.")

The spirituality presented in these pages can be tossed roughly under the category of "New Thought." Now, before you slam the cover shut and drop kick this book across the room, let me hasten to tell you that *New Thought is not New Age*.

The New Age movement is a recent phenomenon that unites under one name a broad spectrum of metaphysical and occult practices that used to be pursued separately. The New Thought movement is over 150 years old in its present form and existed prior to that as *Deism*, a spiritual system that was the "religion" of the great philosophers of eighteenth century Europe and America, including among its adherents Voltaire, Thomas Jefferson and Benjamin Franklin.*

The origin of **I'm Looking for Mr. Right** was my own dissatisfaction with the New Thought movement's response to the AIDS crisis. In the early 80s, I was managing the book store of the Religious Science church to which I belonged. I scanned my distributors' catalogs regularly, searching for books that would be useful to the many gay people in our congregation during what I knew was a very challenging time in their lives. After a while it became clear to me that no one but *no one* was going to write a book about the spiritual causes and spiritual healing of AIDS. I found this particularly galling in that New Thought metaphysics originated as a system for the healing of physical disease through spiritual means and AIDS was perhaps the number one health crisis of the twentieth century. I believed then that the fact of who was getting the disease explained why no one was hurrying to write a book about it. This galled me even more, since I knew how many New Thought ministers were gay men.

---

* For those who are interested in knowing more, there is a history of the New Thought movement in the Appendix.

My complaints about this situation grew increasingly strident until one of my friends became *very* tired of me one day (over brunch somewhere.) In utter disgust, he tossed a forkful of *torte milanaise* back down onto his plate and said, "Well, faggot, why don't *you* write the book!"

I was wrong about why no one was writing the needed AIDS healing book; like much of the general public, none of us New Thought types believed AIDS was going to be around for very long. Back in the mid-80s people were saying things like, "Oh, another five years or so and they'll have a cure." Tra la. We didn't devote much attention to it because we didn't think we'd have to.

Sic transit gloria mundi.

In light of AIDS' continuing influence on gay life—and this is another reason for the expanded edition—I've devoted many more pages to the disease, not only as regards the healing of it, but also as regards how disease-free people can deal with their sick friends, and their dying friends. I've drawn heavily upon my experiences of working with PWAs in search of their healing.

New Thought deals with a lot of very ancient ideas, and so it has become fashionable to say that, "New Thought isn't really new." But it *is* new, in two ways:

1 • It applies the scientific investigation process to spiritual questions, and
2 • It promotes the use of spiritual Truth to systematically produce material results.

New Thought spirituality investigates the great religious mysteries through scientific inquiry: Can we prove there is a God? What is God like? What does He, She or It want from us? What experiments can we perform to verify our theories?

Or, to distill those questions even more:

1 • How does It work?
2 • Why does It work that way? and
3 • How can I work It?

The middle question—Why does It work that way?— is the one that will really stretch your mind.

Also, New Thought encourages people to make practical applications of spiritual Truth; this has become very popular with Americans as we seek to "manifest" or "demonstrate" expensive automobiles, better jobs and really sexy lovers.

There was one consequence I expected to follow the book's publication that *didn't* happen: nobody copied me. I had assumed that a few years after **Mr. Right** was published there'd be an avalanche of wisecracking spiritual books for gay guys with titles like *If All of the Good Ones Are Taken, Does That Mean I'm Not One of the Good Ones?* It never happened. There are now, however, lots of books about the spiritual healing of AIDS. Back in 1986 when I was finishing up the manuscript, the only document available on the healing of AIDS was Louise Hay's audio cassette, and it wasn't exactly greeted with choirs and confetti by the gay intelligentsia. Public attitudes have changed.

Meanwhile, there are millions of gay men in America who aren't HIV-positive and, thanks to their health maintenance practices, probably never will be HIV-positive. I expect they're feeling a bit ignored by now. Perhaps this book will offer them some guidance, and a few laughs.

Many readers will see nothing very spiritual about most of what's written in this book. They'll say it's just common sense. Or nonsense. That's fine, let them call it what they like. It isn't my purpose to sell anyone on any particular religious outlook.

It is my purpose to set you free. Free from what? Free from your own assumptions.

People who involve themselves in self-improvement programs worry a great deal when they catch themselves thinking negative thoughts and they become very concerned about the negative input they get from other people. But our own conscious negativity and the ugly influence of others aren't the things that really cause us trouble. Our troubles proceed from our assumptions. Our troubles are manifestations of the beliefs that are so ingrained in our minds that we no longer notice that we're thinking them, or the beliefs we're so sure are true that we greet with indignation any suggestion that they might be false.

If there is any ulterior intention hidden in this book, it is the hope that reading it will help you to become independent in consciousness, to enable you to find your own wisdom about things, to enable you to decide for yourself what is true and how things need to be for you without reliance on bossy activists with fossilized political agendas or busy givers of weekend seminars who tell you that you're perfect exactly the way you are while they sell you techniques for changing everything about yourself.

It is also my sincere hope that you'll laugh a lot while you read this book. To have one's spiritual teachings ignored can be a kind of status symbol for people in my line of work. But to not get laughs in the right places—terrifying.

Here's the Gay 90s edition of *I'm Looking for Mr. Right*. Enjoy, enjoy. If you have anything you'd like to say to me in response, write. My mailing address is in the front of the book.

— Gregory Flood

Part One

Alone, In the Biblical Sense

Always forgive your enemies. Nothing annoys them so much.

—Oscar Wilde

…a double-minded man is unstable in all his ways…

—James 1:8

Chapter One

Attack of the Breeders

How We Think About Ourselves

Puritanism is the haunting fear that
somebody, somewhere may be happy.

—*H.L. Mencken*

We gay people are raised in a society in which religious authorities tell us we're sinners and damned to Hell, in which psychiatrists tell us we're mentally disturbed and need to be cured, and in which law enforcement agencies tell us we're criminals and should be locked up.

It seems we don't have much room to move.

These gay-hating attitudes are woven into the fabric of our society, and they're drummed into each of us at an early age; words like "faggot" and "homo" are hurled as insults by prepubescent schoolboys who have no idea what the words actually mean, who know merely that a "faggot" is a very bad thing to be.

Some of those schoolboys grow up to be you and me.

———

When our gay sex drives assert themselves at puberty, we've already been exhaustively trained to revile the thing we find ourselves becoming.

It's a grim tribute to the power of this conditioning that closeted gays are able, in their minds, to dance around the question of their sexual preference, always getting close without ever putting their shoe in it for years, or decades, or sometimes even their whole lives, without admitting to themselves that they are gay.

This is the reason why "coming out," the process of announcing one's homosexuality to oneself and to others, is so terrifying for so many gays; we're not only facing hostility from society at large, and shocked rejection by our loved ones, but we're also facing the prospect of becoming something loathsome *to ourselves*. We've accepted society's beliefs about us.

We, too, are homophobes.

———

After the confusion and emotional repression of our teen years, many of us emerge into adult life sexually obsessed and emotionally retarded. Men at ages twenty-five, thirty, forty, or older find themselves going through puppy love and first rejection, emotional crises that our heterosexual schoolmates had the opportunity to experience in their early teens. The psychological terrors of coming out are compounded by the presence of a wife, and perhaps children, or by a homophobic career environment in which homosexuality equals instant job loss.

The people who have appointed themselves the protectors of the nation's morals—every society has lots of them—point to the emotional shakiness of our lives and say, "There! You see?" as if the results of years of negative conditioning somehow proved that the basic premise behind that conditioning was valid—which is rather like burning down a house to prove it was made of ashes.

"Hey, Moe! I'm not me! *I'm* me!"

These aren't *conscious* ideas. These negative beliefs operate without our direct knowledge, subtly informing our conscious thought and shaping our life experiences.

It seems unlikely that these entrenched thought systems would fade away because we have sex every Saturday night and get a subscription to the *Advocate*. Neither volunteer

work for gay organizations nor courageous self-pronounce-
ments nor regular visits to the bars nor reading learned
articles will unlock these dreadful mental manacles. Spiritual problems can't be healed by outward activity, not by
good behavior, not by career success. If that were possible,
then the psychiatrists' couches in this country wouldn't be
filled by successful people who feel that their prosperity is
a fragile mask and by healthy people who cling fiercely to
imaginary problems. Neither would the health spas and
plastic surgeons' offices be crammed with people who believe that they would be loved more if they only looked
different (a miserable notion of love), nor would there be a
booming business in how-to sex manuals for couples who
regard any orgasm milder than a *grand mal* seizure to be the
sign of a failing relationship.

I believe that directed mental work must be done to
eradicate these negative ideas in us. If nothing is done to
eliminate them, then they'll continue to be the foundation of
our thinking and our life experiences. I believe that much of
the self-deprecation, loneliness, fizzled relationships, substance abuse, disease, and suicide among gays is not the
product of the situational particulars of the "gay scene," but
rather the result of an inward conviction on our part that we
are doing something perverted *just in living our lives.* This
isn't an idea we've asked for, but it's an idea we've accepted,
however unawares, and it's an idea we must each consciously reject in order to be free of it.

Gay liberation is, first and foremost, an individual
matter, not a political one.

This isn't to say that there's no value in political activity
and legislative reform. Certainly the refinement and correc-
tion of our laws is of vital importance to the well-being—
indeed, to the continued existence—of the United States and
should be the concern of every citizen. Those people whose
talents lie in bringing about these improvements via legal
action, lobbying, and political service should be given our
love, our praise, our votes, and our money. However, we

must not regard their work as being vital to our own *individual* integrity.

In fact, the real strength of gay political action doesn't come from our activists. It comes from gay people living their lives out of the closet. Without a grass roots constituency of openly gay people to point to, our political activists would have a very tough time making any progress in the halls of congress. If you are simply "out" in your daily life, at work and at home, you're making the most important contribution you can to gay liberation politics.

It would be ludicrous to suppose that we'll all be healthy, loved, and financially successful once a sufficient number of politicians in Washington change their minds about us. The freedom to live as we choose is ours right now, no matter society's attitude towards us. This right can neither be bestowed nor rescinded by legislation. There are many examples throughout history of gay couples living openly as such in the midst of monstrous oppression. It is our belief in the government's authority over our individual lives that gives power to that authority. We have, in Truth, always been free to live as we wished.

Like many minority groups, we've made the mistake of linking personal change to social change. "My life can only be as good as society allows it to be," is the underlying belief. But personal change can happen overnight, or even in a single moment of realization, while social change takes place with grinding slowness across generations. To limit our personal evolution to the speed of social evolution is a lousy strategy. And our lives can prosper and blossom right now far more opulently than our society's defenders of the status quo would ever allow.

Our assumption seems to be that we're perfectly okay and it's society that's screwed up. But, the quality of our lives, no matter what political environment we live in, is always determined by the beliefs and attitudes we keep alive in our minds. Negative social biases and hostile fellow citizens might influence the way we choose to express our freedom, but they can't take it away from us. We can never be deprived of the power to control our own lives.

And that means *never.* Not by anyone or anything.

We can, however, give our power away, particularly if we don't know we have it in the first place.

Other people's attitudes about us will never change until we change our own attitudes about ourselves. We project to other people the image we have of ourselves, and this self-image is always the basis of other people's perceptions of us. To be as dreadfully feared and hated by the public as we are *must require our cooperation mentally.* Somewhere within us the oppressive opinions of straight society must strike a responsive chord in order to do us harm.

The Awful Truth

For centuries the societies in which we've lived have persecuted us on the basis of our sexuality. In banding together for defense, we've been forced to become as obsessed with our sexuality as others are. We've taken on the attitudes of our detractors. The amount of attention that gay men give to the simple fact of their sexual orientation is outrageous.

Your sexual orientation is not a very important part of your psychological makeup. It's a minor consideration that has been blown up into a world issue.

The response might be to say, "But sexual orientation affects every part of your personality." That's true; but then, so does every other aspect of your nature. Each part affects every other part. But there are many other mental characteristics that have a far greater impact, and broader impact, on your life than does your sexuality: for instance, your ability to make friends and form relationships, your ability to set aside personality issues in favor of a greater good, your level of confidence in your own creativity and the extent to which you expect good things to find their way to you.

It's sad to see gay people who want their sexual orientation to be the first thing we know about them. Their hair styles, modes of dress, those cute little baseball hats, keys, gestures, and style of speaking are all geared to announce this one thing, as if their gayness were their most fascinating characteristic (they would have to be very dull people indeed for that to be so).

Your sexual orientation isn't a very *interesting* part of your psychological makeup, either. If someone were to ask you what you considered to be your most interesting characteristics, your sexual nature would probably turn up very far down on the list, if it turned up at all, if you really thought about it.

Suppose someone were to say to you, "The fact of your sexual orientation bores me. It's of little interest to anyone except you." Would you feel that he had said, *ipso facto*, that *you* were boring, that *you* were of no interest?

Gay sex is just plain old sex. It's been around as long as the human race has been around, and yet we act as if it had been discovered recently, by Oscar Wilde, or by a research team out of Cal Tech. It's an old-fashioned, commonplace way to be a person, one that really doesn't require quite so many books, learned articles, and international symposiums.

Few people nowadays would deny that physical ills can be created by mental distress. Every day it seems yet another disease—heretofore considered to be of organic origin—is added to the list of illnesses caused by psychological anguish. Migraine, ulcers, indigestion, high blood pressure, and heart attacks have been joined by bronchitis, hemorrhoids, and some cancers. AIDS is inching its way towards this category, though it will probably never arrive.

All disease begins with a bad idea that has been nurtured in the mind too long. It would sound absurdly Victorian to call the sex urge a disease; but, if we pick that word apart, we get "dis-ease," that is, a lack of ease. And many gay men find themselves burdened with fiercely persistent sex urges that make them profoundly dis-easy.

We somehow intuitively know that our lives depend on love. When we come to perceive our lives as loveless, we become desperately frightened, as if we were being starved to death, or dropped in the middle of a desert, or threatened with violence.

The next time you find yourself getting angry with someone because he's being unpleasant to you, know this: you're becoming angry with him because *he's making it difficult for you to love him.* There is that within you which knows that if you can't love, you'll die. This unpleasant fellow is literally threatening your life.

All mental conditions produce physical manifestations. Sex is the physical outpicturing of love, and the sex urge is the physical equivalent of the spiritual yearning to love.

The need in many gay men to find love is agonizingly intense and, to their own thinking, utterly hopeless. Just so, their sex drive is equally agonizing and equally intense because *it's the exact physical equivalent of their mental craving for love.*

That's why we sometimes feel that if we don't get some sex *we will die.* It's important that we understand what our bodies are really telling us.

When a friend says, "If I don't get laid tonight, I'll die," what he's really saying is, "I've got to get some love in my life, or I'll die."

And he's right: he *will* die.

Sorta True Story #1

"Soon, Dear"

I went to a Fourth of July barbecue in Seattle. It was given by an expatriated Southerner who, using some mysterious tracking ability, had worked up a guest list comprised entirely of expatriated Southerners who'd moved to the Pacific Northwest. I had lived in Atlanta for nine years and was a kind of honorary Southerner; I casually addressed people as "y'all" and used expressions like "I reckon" and "I was fixin' to...." It was an evening of pleasant contradictions: the barbecued chickens were served on china and beers were presented on silver trays.

When it grew dark, we decided that we'd go up to the donut sculpture in Volunteer Park and watch the fireworks, rather than hassle with the crowds at Gasworks Park.

Now, if you've lived in Seattle for any length of time you know that *you can't see the fireworks from Volunteer Park.* That spot offers a grand view of the city, and people gather there in the evenings to watch the sunsets, but the fireworks displays could not be seen from there. Since no one at the party had lived in the city for more than a year, no one knew we were on a fool's errand.

We arrived at the sculpture and found the slope below it filled with families sitting in the dark. The children were all under ten years old. There were ice coolers and picnic baskets and beach blankets. (One member of our party, intimidated by the presence of so much heterosexuality, nervously whispered a warning to maintain "low camp," under the questionable assumption that if we avoided expressions like "Oh, girl," and "fabulous," no one would know we were gay.*)

---

* It's interesting to note that the three gay adjectives all begin with "F": *Festive, Flawless* and *Fabulous.*

It quickly became evident that there'd be no fireworks from this view. We could hear them going off somewhere out in the night.

So, we wandered off through the park. We laid on the grass and had a good laugh over our blunder. We watched little snatches of fireworks that peeked out over the treetops, and we tried to imagine what the whole show must have looked like.

As the energy level of the group began to wind down, we split up in different directions to make our ways home. My splinter group passed by the donut sculpture again.

Nobody had moved.

All those people were still sitting there with their coolers and picnic baskets and blankets and children, staring ahead, doggedly awaiting a fireworks display that had ended fifteen minutes before. The adults had a strained, bedraggled air about them.

"When does it start, Mommy?" said a child nearby.

"Soon, dear," said her mother with a querulous flutter in her voice.

"Heterosexuals are so weird," said one of my friends.

The next day, an assortment of people who'd attended the previous night's party gathered for a late breakfast. We chuckled over the determination of those poor people who'd refused to admit to themselves that they'd planned badly.

"Oh my God!" cried one of the people at the table. We all turned to him in alarm.

"What?" somebody else said.

His eyes were wide: "Guys—you don't think they're *still there,* do you?"

We imagined the slope below the sculpture littered with people in the gray, morning light: hair askew, squinting, their children asleep in their arms, beer coolers full of warm water, staring straight ahead, waiting, waiting, waiting, rather than just admitting to themselves that they'd picked a spot where you couldn't see the fireworks.

Do Your Mindwork
Part 1: Are We Not Men?

1 • Stop making an issue of your sexual orientation

No one is as fascinated by it as you are. It's not the shining star of your personality, it's just an orientation. It doesn't really require national television coverage (Phil Donahue notwithstanding).

This is not to suggest that we keep our sexuality a secret, or that we return to our closets. It's just to say that going on Oprah Winfrey won't make you like yourself more.

Be gay, and enjoy your life. Refuse to allow other people to make an issue out of something that's really not very important to you. Bring your other personal qualities to the fore when dealing with anyone, gay or straight.

Do this: When you're dealing with straight men, *mentally note everything you have in common with them.* Stop harping on your differences. Practice this regularly and you'll be amazed at how alike in their thinking gay men and straight men are. The chasm separating us because of our sexual orientations is a fiction that we and they have created together.

We are all men.*

2 • Never use your sexual orientation as an excuse for your failures.

Your relationship didn't fail because there's "too much promiscuity" in gay life. That landlord didn't refuse to rent to you because he discriminates against gays.

Your relationship failed because *you* did, and that landlord discriminated against *you*, not "gay people." Always put the responsibility for your experiences squarely on your own shoulders, where it belongs.

---

* With this misperception come others, i.e., that gay men are not male chauvinist pigs when dealing with women, or that we aren't racists. We assume that because we are the targets of prejudice, we are incapable of prejudice towards others.

3 • Don't use your miserable past as an excuse for a miserable present.

Your parents hurt you? Your childhood environment was oppressive? Your relationship was a disaster? I'm sorry. That stinks. I know, I've had all those problems.

But what exactly do you intend to do about all that now?

If your mother made you crazy, phooey on her. But if what she did is still pushing your buttons ten years later, who's the fool?

Now, your mother or some other parent may have done more than "make you crazy." You may have been the victim of emotional, physical or sexual abuse. If that's so, you need to open your mouth and talk to someone about it. You may need to consult with a mental health professional.

But the first thing the therapist will tell you is that the problem is no longer what your parents did to you. The problem now resides within you.

4 • Stop being offended by other people's negative attitudes about gays.

You'll never reach a point in your life in which absolutely everybody thinks you're wonderful, so stop wasting energy in resentment.

Everyone is doing his best, no matter how dreary his "best" is. Everyone is progressing through life doing the best he knows how with the ideas he has to work with. *Most people who hate gays have no personal basis for their hatred.* It's simply something they were taught to do, just as we were.

These ugly attitudes can be dealt with easily if we relate to these people out of our intellects instead of our egos. Instead of being offended by these people, get interested in them.

5 • Base your opinion of yourself upon your own observations.

Don't rely on other people to tell you who you are. It'll save you the trouble of getting angry when they tell you you're something you don't want to be.

Your identity isn't some pre-existing package sitting around out there somewhere waiting for you to accidentally happen upon it. Your identity is whatever you decide to be.

Set some standards for yourself.

6 • Understand that your craving for sex indicates a craving for love.

for
Self - Acceptance

I am the creation of a perfect Intelligence that can create only that which is like Itself. It is Infinite Wisdom, Infinite Love, and Infinite Fulfillment. It expresses these qualities through me, as me.

Therefore I know that I am not a mistake. I am not here by accident. My sexual desires are implanted in me by Life with the intention that I express them, easily and joyfully.

I am not perverted and my desires are not dirty. I am not oppressed by the negative opinions of others. I hereby reject and release any negative ideas about my sexuality that I have been taught by others, even the negative ideas taught to me by people whom I loved very much.

I am healed right now of all prejudice against myself.

My desires are clean and wholesome and correct. I embrace them, and I exercise them in good conscience. I am a healthy person who was created on purpose and who is supposed to live happily.

I praise this truth and I allow it to be the foundation of my thinking now and forever.

Chapter Two

I Left My Heart in San Francisco. And Key West. And L.A. And Fire Island. And Provincetown. And I Hear Phoenix Is Nice...

The Search for Mr. Right

A great many people think they are thinking when they are merely rearranging their prejudices.

—*William James*

Humanity has long been obsessed with the idea of Fulfillment as a geographical location. The ancient world abounded in legends of advanced civilizations, always just out of sight, always located in areas that our race had not yet explored. The Greeks and Romans believed in the Hyperboreans ("Far North Dwellers") who lived near the Arctic, as well as Ultima Thule ("Farthest Place"), a magical land similarly located. The Middle Ages buzzed with travelers' tales of the Kingdom of Prester John, the Terrestrial Eden, and the Isle of Avalon. Millions made pilgrimages to miraculous shrines where saints dispensed divine bounty (rather like store clerks selling merchandise owned by the store). "God is not here," people seemed to say about their lives, "but He has a retail outlet over there." This belief, that the grace of God could be reached by boat, helped to inspire the Crusades.

Perhaps these legends later served to explain the savage, amoral rapacity of the European invaders of the newly discovered American continent. There, after centuries of empty legends, was a *real* undiscovered land replete with gold, jewels, haunted forests, scorching deserts, strange pagan tribesmen, bizarre animals, and magical spots like the golden city of El Dorado and the Fountain of Youth. Perhaps those centuries of legends fueled the Europeans' monstrous desire to devour this country whole, church morality—and the native inhabitants—be damned.

In recent times these legends of faraway lands became harder to swallow as the world became better explored and satellites began to take snapshots of the globe from orbit. (One Saturday morning my friend and I were watching "Tarzan and the Lost Volcano" while we drank our coffee. My friend turned to me and said, "What kind of idiot could *lose* a volcano?")

So, we switched our belief in lost lands from "now" to "then." These perfect places used to exist, we said, but they are gone now. Thus Atlantis, and Mu, and Lemuria, all sunk, and the lost magical lore of the Egyptians, and the lost knowledge incinerated in the library of Alexandria.

But believing that these far countries were no longer accessible offended us on an intuitive level, so we transferred our geographical search for perfection to the next available frontier: outer space.

UFOs and Gods from Space have replaced Atlantis, and Prester John, and Ultima Thule. If there are no hidden lands on earth where happiness, wisdom, and abundance are free to all, then, we have reasoned, there must be *planets* where this is so, beautiful planets inhabited by races far older, and wiser, and more advanced than our own. (In the first Superman movie, the advanced state of life on the planet Krypton was symbolized by the absence of chairs; Kryptonians were apparently too highly evolved to sit down.)

Many popular spiritual pursuits reflect this geographical predilection. The shelves of metaphysical book stores are crammed with books not "written by" the author, but rather "channeled through" him. These books allege to be the writings of superior beings, either deceased people or otherworldly, nonhuman entities, who are living in some other-dimensional realm where happiness, wisdom, and abundance are free to all. These entities have the knowledge we need to live well, we are told, and are sharing it with us through the medium of the person writing the book.

Also, astral projection has grown in popularity. Again, the search for truth through this technique is a geographical matter: we must free ourselves from our lumpish material bodies *(sic)* and travel off to other dimensions where happiness, wisdom, and abundance are free to all.

Even Christianity, the dominant religion on this planet, tells us that we once lived in a glorious garden where all our needs were met and where we spent our days in peaceful pursuits. And Christianity offers us the ultimate geographical cure: when we die we'll go to a joyful afterlife in a glittering land called Heaven where happiness, wisdom, and abundance are free to all.

It's all so familiar. Happiness, it seems, is always somewhere else. Therefore, the conclusion becomes inescapable that all an unhappy person needs to do is to move somewhere where happiness is.

Our ancestors with their tales of enchanted lands, our contemporaries with their tales of Close Encounters and sunken continents and their belief in higher entities and ascended masters, and all those millennia of priests who preached the glorious afterlife were all expressing, to the best of their understanding, a spiritual truth: namely, that life is *supposed* to be peaceful, and abundant, and joyful, and beautiful, and fulfilling. They intuitively knew that was the life they should be living; and, since they were clearly not living it where they were, they reasoned that it must be available somewhere else.

And so, the Isles of the Blessed, and the Holy Sepulchers, and Gods in Spaceships.

The only place they failed to look was within themselves. This is especially curious in the case of the Christian clergy, for Jesus clearly stated, in so many words, that the Kingdom of Heaven is within you.

976-LOST

In the early 1970s, a leading gay publication ran an article about two gay men who had been lovers for decades. As the gay Liberation Movement blossomed and gay relationships began to be discussed in a positive manner, these men were frequently called upon to talk about their long-term union at various consciousness-raising seminars.

The question most often asked this couple—and always in tones of anguished frustration—was, "Where did you *meet* each other?"

This question always amused the two because they had picked each other up in a public bathroom. Not real romantic. It also disturbed them, however, in that a large number of gay men apparently thought that there was somewhere one could go where prospective lovers were more plentiful than at other places.

————

Finding a lover, it seems, or even a one-night stand, is directly related to the size of one's field of prey.

I've had many conversations with lonely gay men who were planning to move to some gay Mecca like San Francisco because they thought it would be "easier to meet people there," or who were moving to some city with a smaller gay community like Boston or Seattle because people were "less promiscuous there" (apparently from lack of opportunity).

The famous Religious Science authority Raymond Charles Barker used to answer written, anonymous questions from his audience. Once he received a note stating, "I am unhappy in New York. People are cold to me here. I have no friends. I am moving to Indianapolis."

"Good!" Barker replied to the unknown audience member. "Move to Indianapolis! Maybe somebody will like you *there*!"

The unknown writer has never stepped forward to tell us if his moving plans were changed by Dr. Barker's typically blunt response, but the message to us is clear: *Love is not a location.*

How many times have we sat in groups discussing which bars we go to and why, what kind of crowd goes to which bar, and—most perplexingly—which bars it is easier to get picked up in. (I always wondered what determined that. Better lighting? Worse lighting?)

Now, there's nothing wrong with going out to find some good sex on a cold night. Sex is a great way to make friends, and I've seen it act as a terrific icebreaker at dull parties. However, such action must be undertaken as an exercise in the joy of living, as an expression of the fullness of your life. If sex is undertaken as a means of bolstering up your sagging self-respect, as a salve to your loneliness, or as a means of establishing your status in other people's eyes, you have some serious mental work to do.

You can't have good sex for a bad reason. Your sexuality is no different from your money supply in that you must use it wisely if you expect it to produce good results for you. Use it poorly and, with sex as with money, you will have nothing to show for it finally but bills to be paid.

It's ludicrous, however, to seek love in one spot or another. You'll be "Looking for Love in All the Wrong Places" until you understand that love is not someplace and therefore can't be looked for at all.

The *only* place you'll ever find love is within yourself. If you want your life to be filled with love, then you must fill it with love on your own initiative. If you lack love in your life, then you must be brave enough to stop looking and start loving.

"Start loving who? I'm alone!"

Start loving yourself.

"I do love myself!"
Right.

I often suspect that gay men project their secret images of themselves into their sexual fantasies. I suspect that men who are morbidly attracted to blue-eyed, blond ballet dancers frequently fantasize *being* blue-eyed, blond ballet dancers. And for some gay men, the older they get, the younger their preferred sexual partners become. A man who at the age of thirty was happy with sexual partners in his own age group finds himself lusting for college students by the time he's fifty, and in his sixties gazes longingly at photographs of sultry boys not too long out of potty training.

Who we desire frequently reflects who we want to be; and when we find ourselves desiring people who have nothing in common with us, we're seeing expressed in them qualities that we feel we can never develop in ourselves. The gays who hunger for young, young flesh see themselves as old, old, old. The ones who hanker futilely after beautiful male models consider themselves homely, and the ones who are ashamed of their bodies are always on the lookout for a Sylvester Stallone lookalike to go home with.

We seem to think we can excuse our faults by having a lover who doesn't share them. "It doesn't matter if I'm critical and unpleasant, because my lover is a sweetheart." "It doesn't matter if I drink to excess, and smoke, and overeat, and never exercise, because just look what I get to go to bed with every night." One begins to wonder exactly what this warmhearted, liquor-shunning Olympic gymnast is expected to see in our grouchy, sagging selves.

————

To bring love into your life you must stop looking for Mr. Right and start being Mr. Right.

Finding true love is not a matter of being in the right place at the right time. It's a matter of being the right person all the time. The place will take care of itself.

The place, in fact, will be wherever you are.

Sorta True Story #2

Mom's Rapture

In certain Christian sects there's the belief in something called the Rapture. The Rapture is both a feeling and an event. When the end of the world comes and Judgment Day is nigh, say these folks, those who have allowed Jesus into their hearts will be swept up into the Rapture and carried away into the sky to be gathered to the bosom of God. The event is due any day, we're told. I once saw a bumper sticker that said: CAUTION: I BREAK FOR RAPTURE.

A friend's mother became involved with such a teaching. She worked avidly to convert her family to this new outlook, but they would have none of it.

One day, my friend, who liked his mother very much, called her just to say hello.

"You'd better know this, dear," she said. "The Rapture is coming."

"Oh. It is."

"Yes, it is. So, the next time you call, I may not be here. I just wanted you to know why so you wouldn't worry."

"Uh-huh. Mom, are you sure about this? If I call again and you're not there, it's the Rapture? I mean, between now and the next time I call you're not going to go grocery shopping or get your hair done or take a shower? If you're not there, it's the Rapture?"

"That's correct," she replied with a tone of cool condescension. "But don't worry. I'm sure your *father* will be here to tell you where I've gone."

Do Your Mindwork

Part 2: How to Be Where You Are

1 • Remember that a geographical cure will only solve a geographical problem.

If you live in Oklahoma and your greatest desire is to be a scuba diver, you have a geographical problem. If you live in Oklahoma and you feel friendless and unloved, your problem won't be ameliorated by moving to the ocean.

2 • Have the courage to stop looking for love.

Start to live in a loving manner instead. No one else can fill your life with love. Only you can do that for yourself.

3 • Know that you are Mr. Right.

Examine the qualities in your fantasized Mr. Right and cultivate those qualities in yourself. If these imaginary accomplishments are such that you have no desire to do them—i.e., if your fantasy man is a famous bodybuilder and your idea of exercise is mixing the Bloody Marys before brunch—then you need to reassess your attitude toward yourself. Your low opinion of yourself is causing you to desire a lover who can do all the things you can't. Or won't. You want him to be, like it says on the old movie posters, "everything you can never be!"

Stop focusing on your supposed inadequacies and start to admire what's good about yourself. You'll soon find yourself becoming attracted to men with whom you have something in common, instead of some imaginary creature whose life can never intersect your life in any way.

4 • Never respond negatively to something you want.

The next time you're in a situation where someone is showing sexual interest in you, see if you can catch yourself thinking badly of him because of it. To look down your nose at people because they desire you is not a healthy practice.

I don't know about you, but I want to be attractive. I'm never rude to people who show sexual interest in me, regardless of whether or not I'm interested in them.

Always express gratitude mentally *(mentally!)* to someone who finds you attractive. Practice this regularly and you'll become increasingly attractive to more and more people.

for
A Loving
Life Experience

AFFIRMATION

I am in the presence of Infinite Love right now. Love is the power that runs the universe and it is the power that runs me. I unite myself with it now.

I am designed to be loving and to be loved. Love is my birthright and I accept it now. I allow into my life all people who share my loving outlook, knowing that I always attract those people whose consciousness is most compatible with mine.

There is nothing in me that interferes with the action of love in my experience. I release and reject any unloving ideas or hard attitudes now operating in my consciousness.

I am a living manifestation of love, and I express that nature at all times. My life is full of love because I am filling it with love right now.

I praise the action of love in my mind. I am grateful for all demonstrations of love in my life, and I now release this loving Power to do Its good work for me now, today, and forever.

Chapter Three

Halloween Syndrome
Identity and Disguise

When people are free to do as they please,
they usually imitate each other.
—*Eric Hoffer*

Given that we gay people have come to regard love as something to be searched for some*place*, it's instructive to take a look at the places we've made for ourselves to do our searching in.

————

After the Stonewall Riots in 1969, the focus of the newly minted Gay Liberation Movement was to get us out of the bars and bathhouses and into the sunlight of day-to-day life in America. Within the space of a few years, however, that idea faded away. The bars and baths became larger, more glamorous, and more public, and gay freedom became a matter of being able to go to those places unmolested by police and fag-bashers. The dreary nocturnal lifestyle that we originally regarded as one forced upon us by societal oppression did not fade out as that oppression was lifted. Rather, it became more strongly entrenched.

When a friend of mine was going over some old issues of the *Advocate* that I had around, he made a disconcerting observation: the photographs of the bar scene of fifteen years ago were indistinguishable from similar photographs taken only months ago. Furthermore, the photographs of bar parties in San Francisco, L.A., New York, Atlanta, and anywhere else you care to name all looked the same: the same T-shirts, the same jeans, the same mustaches, the same keys, the same leather, the same bandanas. (A friend who heads a gay S&M motorcycle club once wrote me out a list of what all those different colors mean, in left and right pockets. Bloodcurdling.) The only distinguishing feature was that gay people didn't wear denim knickers in the 70s.

If our night life has changed little in the last two decades, it's because it's based on the same concepts about ourselves that we were using twenty years ago.

Clearly, we need to develop better ideas about who we are. The gays who stood up to the police at Stonewall were acting on a startling new idea: "We don't have to take this any more!" And, as with all great ideas, it swept the country in nothing flat. "Greater than the tread of mighty armies," said Voltaire, "is an idea whose time has come." Suddenly homosexuals all over the country were standing up to the police and saying, "We don't have to take this any more!" Organizations were organized, marches were marched, lobbying commenced, and our legal system has begun to slowly, creakingly change in our favor.

"We don't have to take this any more!" It was, is, a great idea. It was our first great idea, and our last. We have, as a group, been moving forward on that idea for a long time, and I sense our momentum failing. Granted, we don't have to "take this" any more, but what exactly do we intend to "take" instead? We know what we don't want, but what *do* we want?

Now that we're establishing a political environment in which we feel free to live more openly and more as we wish, we seem to be a little at a loss as to what to do with ourselves. We've perpetuated our bar-and-bath lifestyle because we don't have any better ideas.

Gay journalists are forever publishing articles that lament the empty sameness of our social lives. "Why are there no alternatives to the bars?" they cry.

There are no alternatives to the bars because not enough gay people think highly enough of their sexuality to *produce* an alternative to the bars. Our collective environment will never be anything more than a material equivalent of the ideas we hold about ourselves. If those ideas are ugly and self-limiting, then our environment will be ugly and self-limiting. It can be no other way.

Again—and it can't be repeated too often—we're talking about transparent belief systems: ingrained, long-established ideas that inform our thinking so subtly that we fail to recognize their influence.

Alternatives to the bars have been tried: one Chicago group attempted to establish weekly ice cream socials on Sunday afternoons as an alternative to nocturnal bar-hopping. The sight of all those muscle-boys in their tank-tops and cool-dude sunglasses, with thumbs hooked into the loops of their sprayed-on jeans, standing around in Lincoln Park solemnly licking ice cream cones was *too funny.*

We were given an alternative environment, but we came to it with the same ideas about ourselves we'd always had. Result: a gay bar 'neath the elms without liquor. Talk about dull. Everybody finished his ice cream and went to get a drink somewhere.

A new friend once invited me to a party at his condo. He was an archaeologist associated with the local museum of natural history; very brainy, very witty. He told me it was to be an "interesting mix of people," all gay, and that I simply *had* to be there because I had *so* much to offer.

I went to his place on the appointed night, expecting one of those terribly urban, meaningful evenings with all of us discussing art by candlelight on the terrace while drinking wines we'd never heard of before. I was delighted to have somewhere to go to socialize other than a bar.

When I got there, I discovered the place dimly lit, with blasting dance music, and all those "interesting" gay men leaning glumly against the walls, drinks in hand, cruising.

Oh, well. No cover charge anyway.

Each of us carries his consciousness around with him everywhere, and it sets about creating the same experiences for us wherever we go. It's like a good little computer that gives us back only what we've programmed into it.

This is why our problems—and our bad relationships—tend to repeat themselves, no matter what city we move to, and why all those "interesting" men at that party and all the guests at the ice cream social slipped into a cruise-bar mode of behavior automatically even though they had contrived expressly to avoid such an environment.

As children most of us were taught that God gave us free will. Let's interpret this now to mean that Universal Intelligence always says "yes" to our beliefs, no matter what they are. There is no Divine Stock Boy up in the sky who thinks, "Greg believes in thus-and-such, but I know that will generate unhappy experiences for him, so I think I'll ignore that particular belief." Mind always gives to us in terms of what we believe life has to offer. Oscar Wilde, who was a better metaphysician than he knew, said, "When God wants to punish us, He answers our prayers."

However (to refute Oscar), our negative experiences don't come to us as punishment for our shoddy thinking, they come to us simply as a *manifestation* of our shoddy thinking. "Sin" is merely wrong thinking engaged in for too long. And although we're never punished *for* our sins, we're always punished *by* them.

Life always delivers into our experience that which enables us to act out our belief systems. The people in our lives who cause us trouble have been brought to us by Mind in response to our beliefs about life; they're there to help us express our consciousness. We have, in effect, requested them. If someone in your life is giving you a hard time, search out in your mind which of your abiding ideas about life he represents. Replace the bad idea with a good one, and he'll leave you alone; you won't be any fun any more.

We attract our lovers through the same process. If you believe that you must sacrifice your self-respect in order to keep a lover, you'll surely attract someone who'll exact that price from you. If you believe that you can have a stable relationship only by owning your lover, there are lots of very handsome young men out there who are unemployed (or who would like to be unemployed). If you believe that you'll never attract a lover until you're built like the Soloflex man, you'll find yourself in a world full of attractive men who find you totally uninteresting sexually, and a world full of expensive health clubs offering you the solution.

Do you really think you're that undesirable? Do you really think you can't attract a lover until you're so gorgeous you stop traffic? Or until you're rich as Howard Hughes? Does that seem reasonable?

If you suffer from a consistently lackluster love life, your difficulties proceed from beliefs working in your consciousness without your knowledge or consent. You'll carry these ideas around with you everywhere, attracting the same kind of experiences, until you consciously take steps to eliminate them.

The Myth of Adonis

The gyms in my neighborhood are filled with gay men, many of whom are trying to develop magnificent bodies while still maintaining dreary belief systems.

Most of them are still lonely. The more muscular they become, the more bewildered they seem to be. *Does anybody like me yet?* their eyes seem to say. Some gay men are so self-conscious about the physiques they've developed through exercise that they can no longer walk across a room normally. (Remember the scene in *La Cage aux Folles* where Albin learns to walk like John Wayne?)

The strategy here is to create a physical appearance so stupendous that someone will want to have a relationship with you solely because of the way you look. It's an attempt to establish a relationship in which nothing is required of you. It's an attempt to *get* love without having to *give* anything.

Many gay men have never been in a viable relationship and so have a hard time imagining what it must be like. A relationship isn't a situation in which two people "become one"—an unappetizing concept. A relationship is a third party. There is Lover A and Lover B and between them they create a third entity called a "relationship" to which they both must contribute. They do *not* relinquish their individuality; they create something new in their lives, together. And if both parties aren't committed to having the relationship, then there is no relationship, no matter how ideally suited they are in all other particulars.

Obviously, such an arrangement must be an ongoing process of negotiation. Many single gay men falsely assume that long-term couples eventually reach a point in their relationships at which all conflicts have been settled and they can breeze through the rest of their lives in serene harmony. (Very boring.) In fact, successful couples have learned to renegotiate their relationships in a businesslike fashion at regular intervals in response to changes in each other's plans, goals and desires.

The pump-up-your-muscles strategy seeks to bypass the working requirements of a relationship. It's an attempt to use horniness to eliminate the negotiating process. It's based on the belief that problems in the proposed relationship can be smashed flat and destroyed by the sheer force of sexual passion between the two (presumably gorgeous) lovers.

It doesn't work. Two people who decide to build a relationship together can't get by on sexual razzle-dazzle for very long. They've got to roll up their sleeves and get to work on the tough stuff.

Why? Why do they do all that work? Because they want to have a relationship with each other. They do the work because they both desire the result.

And that brings us to the real magic formula for establishing a working relationship. Many gay men get involved in spiritual teachings where they learn that they can create new situations in their lives by changing their thought.

"Believe it and you can have it." Okay, fine. So, they draw up their lists of characteristics for the "perfect" lover they're looking for. He needs to be good-looking, sensitive, supportive, into the same spiritual trips as they, the same politics, same cultural pursuits, same movies, same pastimes and, of course, he must be absolutely *fabulous* in bed.

This is all a crock.*

There's only one qualification you need to seek out in a prospective lover. It is this:

You must find someone with whom you want to have a relationship who wants to have a relationship with you.

That's it. All other considerations are negotiable. Read that passage over a few times, in case it didn't sink in.

Now, this isn't to say that you only need to find someone who "wants to have a relationship." You can turn to the personal ads of any gay newspaper and find dozens, hundreds of gay men who "want to have a relationship." (GWM, HWP, 32, athletic, liberal, fun-loving seeks same for romance and good times. Must love candlelight dinners and walks on the beach. Serious replies only. No fats or fems. Send photo.)

You need to find someone who wants to have a relationship with *you specifically.* Out of everybody in the whole world, he wants to have a relationship with *you specifically.*

And if you can't imagine anyone wanting you specifically out of the whole rest of the world, then you have some work to do on your own self-image before you attempt a relationship. Working on your personal appearance might not be a bad place to start. But it's a lousy place to stop.

And this business of making up a list of characteristics that your "perfect" lover must possess is an attempt to create a relationship in which conflict is impossible or in which all conflicts have been resolved before the two of you ever meet.

---

* It's interesting to note that although such lists always include the item, "He must be supportive of me," they very rarely contain the item, "He must be someone of whom I can be supportive and who will accept my support."

Every gay dance club has its own Golden Circle: that small band of Greek gods with perfect faces and perfect bodies. You know who I mean. They only speak to each other. They dance only with each other. They're the only people in the place who look good in black bicycle pants (though, unfortunately, they're not the only people in the place *wearing* black bicycle pants.) Their demeanor makes it very clear that to enter into their social set requires very specific credentials, the principle one of which is that you look good in black bicycle pants.

These are the people everybody stares at all night long. These are the people everybody fantasizes about later on in the evening after going home alone and horny. To know one of these people is a status symbol. To get one into bed is a major social victory. To have one for a boy friend, well, the party invitations would never stop coming.

Have you ever wondered, if these guys have such exciting, successful love lives, why they're always standing around in bars just like you are?

After the first version of this book was published, word got around that the author worked as a practitioner at the local New Thought church. Many clients came to see me on the strength of what they'd read and, lo and behold, among them were the members of our local Golden Circle. And I was astonished to discover that these bronzed Adonises had the same problems that all my other gay clients had: loneliness, an inability to make connections with people, a feeling that no one knew who they really were, a sense of hopelessness about ever finding a lover.

Live and learn.

What all those health club members were trying to develop, the Golden Circle members already had, and it didn't get them any of the things it was supposed to get them. They experienced only the contents of their consciousness just like everybody else.

Now, there's nothing at all wrong with wanting to have a beautiful body. We must always cultivate beauty in ourselves in all ways, including our physical appearance. Our clothing and hair style should be appropriate to our self-image. If you feel your gray hair is unattractive, color it. If you've gone bald and don't like it, there are ways of fixing that. If your face sags too much, get it lifted.

Just be aware that altering your appearance will improve only the way you look. It won't make you rich, creative, loving, or loved.

Furthermore, you'll still be operating from a consciousness that believes that your appearance determines the quality of your life. And, as your mind naturally continues to expand, it will begin to manifest a very natural dissatisfaction with things as they are, and you'll find new physical flaws on which to lay the blame.*

Trying to ease your loneliness by altering your appearance is like trying to save a burning building by putting in new carpeting. Solving your spiritual problems through material means is an endless process. Until the underlying ideas are changed, there will always be more of the problem to work on.

Before deciding how you want to look, you must first decide who you are. Then, if you still desire a change in your appearance, you'll make that change for the right reason— to express who you are, not to change who you are—and not to create the impression that you are someone that you aren't, and not to build an identity for yourself from the outside in.

———

This obsession with how we look is the product of a lifestyle in which pickup bars are the principal social outlet. The strategy engendered by these places is that the more alluring we look the greater chance we have of "meeting people" (as we euphemistically refer to "getting laid"), and the more love, excitement, and satisfaction we'll produce in

---

* One person of my acquaintance decided that the solution to his chronic loneliness was to go to a plastic surgeon for a gluteal augmentation. A butt job. For years afterward, people would look at him and say, "Who is that sad little man with the magnificent ass?"

our lives. This is predicated on the belief that the interaction in bars is a matter of bodies lusting after other bodies.

Know this: *the cruising in gay bars is entirely and only a matter of consciousness seeking out compatible consciousness.* Your appearance may get people's attention, but who gravitates to you and who you meet and go home with is entirely due to your consciousness, to your deep-set, transparent ideas of what life must be for you.

If your expectations of love always include disappointment and pain, you will surely attract just the right people to produce that for you. If you expect to achieve nothing with your cruising, you will attract no one.

That's why so many gorgeous people go home alone, or go home with people who care nothing for them as individuals. It's also why so many truly homely people seem to attract such spectacular bed partners. And it's why so many really pleasant, respectable-looking, intelligent, creative people go home lonely, night after boring night.

Many a gay man of my acquaintance over the years has complained to me bitterly that the people he encounters are "too shallow," and that people would appreciate him more if they would only see through the surface to the "real him."

"Nobody understands who I really am!" seems to be a cry on the lips of many gay men. Perhaps you repeatedly make this complaint yourself.

Well, you're wrong.

They *do* know the real you. They see you clear as day, frequently more clearly than you care to see yourself. That sounds very harsh, I know. Ralph Waldo Emerson put it more gracefully in his essay *Spiritual Laws:*

> Human character evermore publishes itself. It hates darkness—it rushes into light....If you act, you show character; if you sit still, you show it; if you sleep, you show it.
>
> Dreadful limits are set in nature to the powers of dissimulation. Truth tyrannizes over the unwilling members of the body.

> A man passes for what he is worth. Very idle is all curiosity
> concerning other people's estimate of us, and idle is all fear of
> remaining unknown.

Most communication between people takes place below the surface of appearances. The most important messages we send out and receive penetrate all our disguises, all our subterfuges, and override any flattering illusions we wish to project about ourselves. (Have you ever been introduced to someone and, for no apparent reason, instantly distrusted them? Have you ever notice that a person can sense that you're looking at him, even if his back is turned? Have you ever wondered how it is that gay men can recognize each other as such at a glance?)

It may strike you as an alarming idea that anyone can see through the masks you choose to wear, but this knowledge has its comforting side: nobody can fool you either.

Unless, of course, you let them.

How many gay men have we seen move in with some nasty, unsuitable lover, despite all our pleadings and warnings, simply because nobody else seemed to be interested in them just then? They so wanted to be able to live with someone, to have at least the appearance of a happy relationship, at least for a short while.

It is said that appearances can be deceiving. This is patently false. Appearances are deceiving only to him who wishes to be deceived, or who is already deceiving himself.

Sorta True Story #3

What He Died Of

This is a story about alcohol, but you can apply it to a lot of different issues.

Old Callahan died and there was a wake. He was laid out there with his widow, a sad old Irish lady, standing by the coffin.

Widow Dolan walks up to her: "Ah, Widow Callahan. What did he die of?"

Widow Callahan sighs deeply. "Ah, Widow Dolan. He died of the drink."

"The drink!" cries the other. "Oh, why didn't you take him to Alcoholics Anonymous?"

Widow Callahan's eyes go wide and she raises herself up with fierce indignation. "Ho!" she says. "It was never that bad!"

Do Your Mindwork
Part 3: Cruising Tips for Spiritual Guys

We're supposed to be living in an era of unbridled sexual license, but everybody secretly knows this isn't true. Most gay guys haven't gotten laid since disco was king.

This isn't for lack of trying. With all the effort expended by gay people in the search for sex, you'd think more of us would actually *get* some. But no. The reason our news and entertainment media are so inundated with sexual imagery is because people aren't getting any; if gay people had fulfilling sex lives, we wouldn't look twice at Calvin Klein ads or talk shows about male strippers. We're fascinated by that stuff because we never see any of it in our bedrooms.

You'd think, with all the time and energy we put into looking for sex, that we'd be better at finding it. But even after years of looking for it, most gay men are as inept in their search procedures as if they'd just hit puberty. Here's a few helpful metaphysical hints for improving your sex life.

1 • Everyone knows what you're doing.

There's nothing funnier than someone trying to look like he's not cruising when he's cruising. People have a seemingly inexhaustible repertoire of covert surveillance techniques. In fact, most gay men who are looking at you in a public place will look away if you look back at them, as if they are afraid you'll know they're cruising you and want to go to bed with you, even though they *are* cruising you and *do* want to go to bed with you.

There's only one Mind, and we all think with It. When you're looking for sex, everyone knows what you're doing because they're all thinking with the same Mind that you are. So, quit all that nonsensical sidelong staring and reflection-in-the-window watching. Be honest. You might as well be; everyone knows what you're doing anyway.

2 • Being attracted to someone is fun in itself

You don't have to consummate every sexual impulse that possesses you. Don't even try: they'll throw you out of the laundromat forever. Being sexually attracted to people is one of the great pleasures of life. Don't turn it into a burden by insisting that every sexual impulse culminate in a sexual encounter. The people you find sexy need never know about your feelings; those feelings are for you to enjoy.

3 • The desire for sex will pass whether you have sex or not

This is also true of the desire for a cigarette, the desire for dessert or the desire to punch someone. We don't have to carry through on a desire to be rid of it; we only need to wait.

4 • If you want your sex life to work, make sure your life works.

Your bodily desires are expressions of the aspects of your consciousness: your desire for love, for peace of mind, for connectedness, for success. Our sexuality can become perverted or frustrated when other aspects of our experience are out of order. Sex becomes an inappropriate substitute for whatever we feel is missing from our lives. If you're experiencing dissatisfaction of any kind with your sex life, the solution may not be more sex or a different kind of sex. The solution may be to devote time and energy to the improvement of the other areas of your life that aren't satisfactory to you.

5 • God loves sex

The Spirit that created you created all your inborn desires and It rejoices in their expression. Many people have terrible sex lives because their minds are filled with transparent negatives: sex is materialistic and dirty, sex cheapens the participants, sex is intended by God to be reserved for a certain kinds of permanent relationships and for certain practical purposes, sex distracts us from the higher realms of spiritual Truth, and so on.

But matter and Spirit aren't separate things. Spiritual Truth isn't in some "other realm" out there. It's right here. It's everything you see, and It's you. *Participation in the world is participation in God's Presence.*

Not only is sex a good thing, but it's perfectly all right, from a spiritual perspective, to desire sex for no practical purpose, just because it feels good. And we can discard any notion about sex being legitimate only within the boundaries of God's rules, because God doesn't make rules.

6 • If you hate the bars, don't go.

"Don't go?!"

Yeah. *Don't go.*

Stop being part of the problem. Don't worry about "meeting people." There are gay guys all over the place just longing to get "met." (How well did you fare at the bars in that regard anyway?)

For your own mental health you must stop exposing yourself to an environment that you despise; it's spiritual suicide. You're not alone in your distaste for the bars: many gays never go to them, or go but rarely. You'll never be able to create a new social environment for yourself until you let go of the old one.

In that same vein, never have sex with anyone you're not really attracted to, and never use drugs or alcohol out of a sense of social obligation.

In other words, enjoy the experiences you want, not the ones people randomly offer you.

7 • There's really nothing you need to become in order to attract a relationship.

You don't need to be rich, or young, or stunningly beautiful, or tops in your field.

You need to be happy with who you are.

As you develop your own capacities, your ideas on Mr. Right will grow and change. Decide what you want in a lover. Set some standards for him and for yourself.

Never consider what you "need" in a lover. You need nothing. Your lover should fulfill your requirements, not make up for your limitations.

8 • You must find someone with whom you want to have a relationship who wants to have a relationship with you.

9 • Develop your personal appearance so that it expresses who and what you are.

Don't develop your personal appearance for the purpose of sexually exciting everyone who looks at you. It doesn't work, and it will make you a nervous wreck.

10 • Never complain that nobody knows the real you.

They do.

for
Self - Expression

AFFIRMATION

I am the creation of an Infinite Mind that already has everything It wants. There is nothing I have that It needs, nor can anything I do please It or disturb Its pleasure. It is infinitely fulfilled, and It produced and maintains this universe as an expression of Its own joy.

I am an expression of that Perfect Joy and I now partake of Its fulfillment. Mind has already given me everything I require to live as I please. All I need do is accept these gifts lovingly and they will burst forth into my experience. All the wealth, creative fulfillment, physical perfection, and love that I require are granted me in every particular right now.

There is nothing in me that obstructs this flow. I hereby release and reject any ideas about my own unworthiness, or any belief that Life is displeased with me and is withholding Its goodness until I perform some act of penance.

There is no withholding in Spirit. Its love for me is unqualified. I am the beloved of the Infinite and It bestows all of Its qualities on me right now, through me, as me, by means of my thoughts and experiences. I effortlessly attract to myself all that is best for me.

I praise the Infinite Mind that has given everything to me, I thank It for Its unending abundance, and I accept all of Its beautiful gifts, now and forever.

Chapter Four

Second Star to the Right and Straight On Till Morning

The Dream of Community

One more indispensable massacre of Capitalists or Communists or Christians or Heretics, and there we are in the Golden Future.

—Aldous Huxley

When someone thinks of himself as a victim he almost never morally evaluates himself or questions his own actions.

—Thomas Friedman

When I'm seated at dinner with a group of gay men, the question arises more often than not, "Is there really such a thing as the gay *community?*" The question is usually put in a tentative tone of voice as if the questioner isn't sure how the others will react.

The answer, in every case that I've witnessed, has been a resounding "No." The gay men I've heard discuss this matter have all to a man either flatly denied the existence of the gay "community" or have at least felt that if there was a gay community out there somewhere, they certainly weren't members of it. This is a conversation I've heard repeated over and over in cities all across the United Stated by gay men from a wide variety of backgrounds.

In every instance I witnessed, this conversation had a hushed and furtive atmosphere about it, as if the participants were afraid of being overheard.

Who, I wondered, were they afraid would hear them?

Something else was clear in listening to these men: they would never voice such an opinion in public. This was a matter to be discussed only behind closed doors. In fact, were they ever to be questioned on the subject in public, they would dutifully nod their heads and say how wonderful it was to be a part of the gay community, rather than risk a confrontation by saying what they're really thinking.

I report this because I've heard the point of view voiced by so many different people in so many different places. Apparently this opinion is held in secret by many gay men, though it's almost never given a public forum.

Why not?

————————

There appears to be a bizarre gap between the way gay men experience life and the way their lives are described in the gay press. To read it in the gay papers, gay men are politically active, threatened at every turn by bashers, radically sexual, constantly in danger of being infected with HIV and part of a network of intense friendships and personal relationships that give their lives color and warmth. Whereas at the level of daily life, many gay men are as indifferent to politics as are any other Americans, move about freely and without any sense of danger beyond the usual city dweller's street smarts, get laid about once every solar eclipse, are not and probably never will be HIV-positive and are so alone in the world that they cry themselves to sleep at night.

This isn't to say that the problems of gay people don't exist (except maybe the problem of too much sex, from which few gay men of my acquaintance seem to suffer): gay bashings are on the rise and the disease called AIDS is appearing in an appalling number of people. But I suggest that, beyond the *factual accounts* of this incident or that incident, the gay news media presents a *world view* that needs to be questioned by thoughtful people.

And if you don't think that's so, watch the 6:00 news every night for a month, all the while affirming, "This is real.

This is what the world is like." At the end of thirty days you'll
be packing a gun in your lunch box, walking from room to
room with a fire extinguisher under your arm, coordinating
your wardrobe to avoid gang colors and refusing to ever get
on an airplane again.

Many gay men seem to have identified themselves with
experiences that they're not having. They've been told that
since they're gay, this is what life is like for them. And they
believe it, lack of evidence notwithstanding.

We could question whether or not most gay men possess the interpersonal skills necessary to maintain a community.

Throughout their adolescent years, most gay men live in
a network of fake relationships. The average gay teenager
pretends to be someone he's not in order to please his
parents, his teachers, his friends and his real or potential
enemies. Nobody really gets to know him very well because
all his interpersonal relationships are based upon a carefully
crafted illusion of shared heterosexuality.

Perhaps this is why the stereotypical gay occupations
are things like hairdresser, fashion designer, interior decora-
tor, artist, writer, actor; all these occupations involve *the
creation of illusions and appearances for the purpose of
pleasing onlookers.* The creation of false impressions is
certainly something that most gay men are very good at after
eighteen years in their parents' homes.

It's a little disingenuous to think that these masters of
hide-and-go-seek can stumble out of their closets and into
adult life, raise their fists over their heads and shout, with
any credibility at all, "Now we shall be a community!" To
create and participate in a community would take relationship-building skills which they haven't had the opportunity
to develop. To forge a community takes a great deal more
than one shared characteristic like sexual orientation. It
requires a mutual outlook that goes beyond politics, and a

shared cultural background like that of African-Americans and Native Americans or a shared language like that of the American Deaf Community. It's questionable to think that a group as diverse as gay people—coming as we do from every stratum of life in this society—can casually form a community based on shared sexual orientation and a history of victimization.

Community-building requires the ability to communicate clearly and to cooperate with others. At the very least it requires that the individual members of that community have a clear idea of who they are as individuals. A "community" made up of confused, argumentative, lonely people who have trouble making connections with each other is no community at all; it's merely a proposed community, an idea of community, a theory.

It's unlikely that you'll ever be able to help forge a community if you've been unable to create a network of healthy relationships in your own life. In the hundreds of gay men that I've counseled over the years, the number one problem in most of their lives has not been AIDS-related; most HIV-positive people I've met have taken their diagnosis in stride and have learned to deal with it intelligently long before they ever came to see me. Neither is it fag-bashing; many men who've been openly gay for their whole adult lives have never heard so much as a harsh word about their sexual orientation from anyone.

The number one problem of almost every gay man I've ever counseled is *loneliness.*

More specifically, the problem is *an inability to make lasting emotional and personal connections with other people.* Perhaps as a result of their closeted adolescence, gay men seem to have a painful and frustrating lack of relationship-building skills. Even the simple act of introducing oneself to a stranger at a social gathering becomes a complex and unnerving reconnaissance maneuver around our secret needs, fears, demands and questions. We don't enjoy simply meeting another human being because we're too busy worrying if our time is being wasted. If we're sexually attracted to the person in question, several layers of subtext are added to the mix since we're then also wondering if he might be...THE ONE. The logic in such encounters seems to be, "All right, look, I know you're going to reject me, so let's get this over with so I can get on to the next prospect." The notion that this new person might become a friend or that he might just be pleasant to talk to for a few minutes is not a consideration.

People who suffer from this kind of emotional neediness are usually not much use to anyone else. They generally take what they can get out of any situation and then leave without so much as a thank you. Many gay entrepreneurs who announce, with stars in their eyes, that they intend to serve an exclusively gay clientele, end up feeling mistreated and abandoned by the alleged community they sought to serve.

Many gay men resort to a kind of "fake friendship": they have a small group of other gay men, maybe only one gay man, who they hang around with not because of any mutual connection between them, or shared interests, but rather because if they didn't hang around with each other they'd each be completely alone. It's not unusual for such friendships-of-convenience to be forged between gay men who, truth be told, don't really enjoy each other's company. A person in such a social arrangement finds that the other participants vanish from his life without a trace as soon as they find prospective lovers.

This isn't friendship, of course. This is a kind of pot luck volunteer escort service that protects all involved from having to appear in public alone.

And if we were to observe the behavior of gay men in public, it would be easy to form the opinion that we don't like each other very much. We certainly don't treat each other very well. And, it seems, we trust each other not at all. And building emotional bridges that connect you to other people requires vulnerability, and the assurance that your vulnerability won't be abused.

Within the hearts of gay men there is clearly a deep *longing* for there to be a gay community. But any such community must be comprised of individuals who are already successful in establishing meaningful contacts with the people in their immediate lives.

The Good Old Days

People aren't lonely because they're alone. They're alone because they're lonely. Loneliness isn't an unfortunate circumstance created by psychological problems and bad luck. Loneliness is a way of relating to the world. Loneliness is a mental attitude. Or, to put it less charitably: *Love is a form of work, and loneliness is a form of laziness.*

To create a loving environment in which to live takes work. It takes *practice.* To live in an environment of love requires us to expend the effort daily, moment by moment, to create positive relationships with everyone we contact. It's not effortless.

It may seem a little silly to establish a healthy and loving relationship with the attendant at the dry cleaners or the person who delivers your mail. But the truth is that you already have a relationship with these people. If you treat the dry cleaning attendant like a human vending machine, as a function, and disregard his humanity entirely, that will be the basis of your relationship; he will have a particular attitude towards you and it's unlikely that he'll ever be especially glad to see you. Even if he performs his function efficiently and you never complain about anything, your relationship will nevertheless be one of dreary indifference, or perhaps sullen hostility. People insist on being treated like people. When you interact with them without at least a tip of the hat to their humanness, they don't like you.

Who *cares* if you have a good relationship with the mailman or the dry cleaners' employee? You care. Or you ought to. You see these people all the time. They're part of your environment. You'll experience your relationship with them, whatever it is, over and over and over.

People love to complain about the lousy service you get nowadays. Nobody does it right any more, they say, nobody cares about doing the job well for its own sake. These complainers sigh wistfully at the covers of the Saturday Evening Post or at Pepperidge Farm commercials on TV which depict a time in our country's past when shopkeepers were warm and considerate and knew their clientele by name. They don't consider the possibility that the lousy service you get nowadays has as much to do with the customers as with the employees.

At the turn of the century, moving around was difficult and inconvenient. People stayed in one place for their whole lives. A shopkeeper in a small community, or even in an urban neighborhood, knew he'd be serving the same clients forever. He couldn't treat them with blank anonymity and expect to stay in business. Furthermore, the customers knew that they'd be accepting service from that same store for the rest of their lives and so they were polite and pleasant in their dealings there; they knew that if the relationship were to turn sour, they'd be stuck with it permanently. The elaborate formality in everyday situations that we perceive in the communities of the past wasn't the result of moral conservatism; it was a practical necessity for living in the same place for sixty or seventy years. You had to get along with people.

The easy mobility of modern life has created a new milieu. We are now afforded the freedom to be unknown. In fact, it's considered quite normal in this society to remain entirely anonymous to people who you see every week for years. Nobody seems to think this is strange.

Many people who complain about the anonymity of modern life, particularly city apartment dwellers, have never bothered to introduce themselves to their neighbors. They don't think it's peculiar to share a wall with another person and know nothing about them. People complain about their lack of connection to others when there are plenty of "others" within easy reach on either side of their apartments.

This isn't to say that you should necessarily become

great pals with your neighbors. Friendship is far more than a matter of geographical proximity. But to live in close quarters with another person for years without once inviting him in for coffee is very weird.*

The network of small-but-crucial personal relationships that characterized turn-of-the-century life can be recreated in a modern environment. But to do so requires a clear sense of purpose in the individual who wants it. And it requires practice.

We resent the idea that love requires effort. We're perfectly willing to accept the fact that if we want a beautiful body then we must exercise and monitor our food intake, or that in order to prosper we must apply ourselves, or that to play a musical instrument we must rehearse. But we're offended by the notion that love takes work. We expect love to be automatic, a kind of permanent hormonal reaction.

Perhaps this attitude is the result of growing up in a family unit whose members are tacitly expected to give each other love and support simply on the basis of their shared biological connection. But in adult life in a highly mobile society, personal connections can be made only with effort. And personal relationships, especially marriage, are only *maintained* through effort.

---

* In my own apartment building, the neighbors all know each other by name. We greet each other pleasantly on the street, keep an eye on each other's apartments when someone's out of town, take in each other's mail and trade off gardening equipment for our individual back yards. The person with whom I share a wall feeds my cats when I'm away and I likewise feed her goldfish. None of us are really good friends, but we are good neighbors.

Sorta True Story #4

Bad Neighbor Sam

Here's a story about someone who created his own community: Like many gay men, Sam complained of his inability to make connections. He had no lover and not many friends. And he didn't really like his friends. He was cordial enough with his fellow employees at the job, but he knew that those connections would be severed when he moved on from there. He watched a lot of TV. He went to museum showings by himself. He was very lonely and very angry.

As we talked in our first session together, it became clear to me that he had a rather low opinion of other people. It made me wonder who he planned on being friends with, exactly, since he didn't seem to like much of anybody. People, he said, were indifferent, and weird, and self-centered, and hypocritical, and obsessed with shallow things, and generally too thick-headed and materialistic to understand someone as complex and metaphysical as him.

This is person-in-counseling talk. It means, "Please help me!"

When I asked if he'd ever introduced himself to his neighbors in the apartment building, he looked at me like I was insane. To hear him tell it, he had the Munsters on one side of him and the Addams Family on the other.

"When you pass people on the street," I asked him, "how do you relate to them?"

"You mean, like, people I've been to bed with?"

I sighed. "No, I mean people you don't know at all. Strangers."

"Well, I don't 'relate' to them."

"You don't. You mean, if you're walking down a street in your neighborhood and there's only one other person in sight coming towards you, in the full minute it takes for you to approach and pass each other, you just keep your head down and ignore him?"

He scowled. "What should I do? Take him out to dinner?"

"You could say, 'Hello.' Or you could smile at him."

"Why should I smile at him?"

"Because he's there. Or because he's a human being who wants essentially the same things you want: a nice place to live, someone nice to live there with, a body that doesn't betray him, a source of income that brings him pleasure, a few stimulating diversions. Out of respect for the fact that he's *survived* this long. Why? How do you think he'll react if you say something to him?"

"He'll think I'm a weirdo. Or that I'm coming on to him."

"Are you sure? Are you absolutely certain about that?"

The day after our consultation, Sam made a decision: he'd try the smiling thing.

So, as he went out to run his morning errands, he smiled—very briefly—at anyone he passed on the street. He didn't *feel* like smiling, he just did it; he performed a mechanical function called smiling. He'd turn away immediately after. The first few times, it must have looked like a death rictus.

Almost everyone he smiled at smiled back. A few people said, "Hello." The more he did it, the easier it got. He very quickly discovered that he had something in common with those people he passed on the street: they all lived in the same area and they all pretty much liked it there. He also noted that many of the people who passed him on the street were the same people who served him in the stores.

This had an unexpected effect on Sam: it made him feel like he belonged where he was. By greeting the people he passed on the street, he very quickly came to feel like he had taken possession of the streets where he walked. This was *his* neighborhood.

As he began to feel more at home where he was—and,

not incidentally, more at home with himself—he found that it was very easy to be friendly and relaxed with store clerks, post office workers, policemen, bus drivers, even panhandlers. He also found that it didn't matter if not all of them returned his kind regard. He still smiled even at the people who kept their heads down as they passed.

And this led to another discovery: he could get through a whole day without acting like a jerk. All of his small-but-crucial relationships were positive. Nowhere in his life did he insult people by treating them as anonymous functionaries. In response to this, he usually got cheerful and, if not efficient, at least well-intended service wherever he went. The cashiers at the grocery store didn't ask if he wanted paper or plastic because they remembered his preference. The dry cleaners would rush things for him at no extra charge. Bus drivers would remember him and ask how he was. The clerks at the video store would set aside tapes that they knew he wanted to see.

As he passed more and more days without having to act like a jerk, Sam found that it began to affect his job performance. He came to work in good spirits. He no longer felt that his job was an imposition on his time. He actually began to enjoy the company of his co-workers.

None of this sounds particularly earth-shaking, because it isn't. But don't miss the point: *this guy lives in a Pepperidge Farm commercial.* All that corny, old-world stuff about friendly, courteous storekeepers who know you by name and fellow citizens who tip their hats to each other, it's all in place in his life. Right here in the supposedly cold and hostile modern world. I'd like to tell you that Sam went on to assemble a dazzling group of friends and that he found his soulmate, but that's not what this story is about. This man learned one of the essential truths about successful living: Love isn't hard to find. Love is *impossible* to find.

Because love isn't something you go out and find. Love is something you express.

Big Sister Is Watching You

In the early 1970s, the term used to describe the new crusade for equal rights for homosexuals was called the Gay Liberation Movement. Gay life was referred to as the Gay Subculture. The term "Gay Community" was around but was used less frequently. In the course of that decade, "community" completely eclipsed the other terms as our description of choice. Perhaps it was easier for gay political activists to present themselves at the centers of government as representatives of a gay community than as representatives of a movement or a subculture. A community sounds so much more respectable and, well, *significant.*

Having coined the term, we've spent the last twenty years browbeating each other into becoming the community that we decided we already were. The results have been indifferent, and the choice of rhetoric has caused problems for many gay people who feel more like outsiders than ever.

While at a seminar engagement in another city I participated in an outdoor gay rally that attracted a sizable chunk of the gay population. The event was MCed by a popular comedian much-appreciated by the gay locals.

As he vamped his way through the afternoon, filling the gaps in the (seemingly endless) array of speakers, he made note of the wide variety of gay people in attendance: male, female, black, white, brown, yellow, red, old, young, rich, poor, Democrat and...but then he stopped.

"Well," he said in an exaggerated manner, "it's hard to imagine a gay Republican." This quip inspired stupendous laughter from the audience, perhaps the loudest and most sustained laughter he'd generated that day.[*]

One person who pointedly didn't laugh was the man seated next to me, another guest speaker, who was president of that state's long-established gay Republican organization which had several hundred members. When he was introduced later, the audience blushed in unison.

---

[*] Since that time, gay people have come out loudly within the Republican party.

The incident was not only an insult to this man, but more important, it hurt his feelings. (Liberals think conservatives have no feelings while conservatives think liberals have *too many* feelings.)

Now, whatever opinion you might have of this man's political views—and I might have a few myself—it's still significant that the idea of a gay Republican incited laughter, as if such a thing was too ridiculous for words. Everybody knows that all gays are liberals, right?

Despite our constant assertion that gays come from every part of society—an assertion that gives our liberation movement much of its credibility—we tend to assume that gay people are all remarkably similar in their points of view. We're perfectly willing to accept the idea of gay people adhering to *religions* that are ferociously homophobic—we consider that it is their right to participate in whatever faith they choose—but we just as casually assume that all gay people share the same *political* outlook. We are assumed to be anti-nuke, pro-abortion, anti-big business, pro-trees and so on. God help the gay man who criticizes the welfare system or supports the rights of the timber industry.

Beyond assuming that we all have the same point of view, there is among many gay activists the idea that we're *required* to have the same point of view. The idea seems to be that we gay people are beset on every side by hostile external forces and that for the sake of survival we must present a united front to the oppressive outside world.

In one city a few years ago, one item in the published political agenda for the annual Gay Pride Week was "an end to the oppression of labor unions." This entry—in a list of otherwise gay-related demands—was a mystery to all the people I questioned about it, including a couple of the event organizers who supposedly helped to compose the document. Leaving aside the issue of whether gay activists should be permitted to inject their other, not-specifically-gay causes into the proceedings of a gay event (and thus to shanghai all who participate or attend into a kind of automatic support, regardless of their political leanings), there is the larger issue represented by the assumption that there are no company management executives who are gay, only gay union workers; which is to say, no gay power figures, only an oppressed gay proletariat. At the very least, the inclusion of this entry on the political agenda for Gay Pride Week implied that if there *were* any gay management executives, they certainly shouldn't feel at home at the Gay Pride Festival; they might be gay, but they were being gay the wrong way.

Whereas a movement can have more branches and appendages than a Third World municipal government, all taking off in their own separate directions and with their own separate agendas, a community requires solidarity in order to preserve itself. For the good of the community, a consensus must be reached and supported by its members. Ranks must close. A community posture toward the outside world must be adopted.

I suggest that by identifying ourselves as a community rather than as a political movement we have created an environment that suppresses diversity of thought and demands that the same values be adopted by all gay people. Perhaps that's why my dinner companions expressed their reservations about the existence of the gay community in such a secretive fashion. They were afraid that some scowling activist would overhear, leap up, point an accusing finger and shout, "TRAITOR!" (As if homosexuality was a *country* that could be betrayed instead of a sexual orientation that can be expressed in an broad spectrum of lifestyles.)

If this is so, it's a sad turn of events, since a community must necessarily exclude at least a few people, whereas a movement can accommodate just about anyone; even the most impossible, contentious crank can make room for himself in a movement simply by creating his own branch of it. A Gay Rights Movement is something to which any gay person could contribute regardless of his political, social or religious affiliations. It would be a place where the gay union organizer and the gay management executive could find common ground with each other; even if they were unable to find anything else in common, they could both at least agree that any prejudice against either of them on the basis of sexual orientation was unacceptable. But a community is something you can get thrown out of.

Although we gay people demand the rights that are the birthright of any citizen of a free society, it seems that our proposed gay community is *not* a free society. We seem to believe there is a kind of gay College of Cardinals out there somewhere that decides what the rest of us are to think if we wish to remain Gay People in Good Standing.

Which raises the curious matter of who's out there making these policy decisions. Articles in gay and mainstream publications often refer to "the leaders of the Gay Community," as in "The conference was attended by leaders of the Gay Community from all over the United States." But what does that mean, exactly?

The vague assumption amongst many gay people is that there is some kind of well-organized, structured network of political activists out there somewhere who have regular meetings with lots of parliamentary procedure to decide the direction of the gay community's future. Anyone who actually knows any such activists knows them as harried, overworked, under-financed people who barely manage to hold their own against resistance from the representatives of government on the one hand and, on the other, indifference from the gay people whose freedoms they try to defend. Such activists do belong to chartered gay rights organizations and those organizations do have leaders; but it's hard to perceive our activists as "leading" us all forward into the future in some kind of stately procession, like Washington crossing the Delaware. They're much too busy for that. And if you factor in how much time and energy gay political workers expend in arguing with *each other* about items of policy, it really becomes impossible to believe in some *ad hoc* gay summit meeting out there that enacts regulations and legislates principles of belief for the rest of us.

We certainly ought to admire these people and be grateful for what they do. They're very important to us. But it's questionable to refer to them as "leaders of the gay community." Who do they lead? Are they your leaders? Are they mine? How do you get to be our leader? Who put them in office? Do we have gay elections? I would certainly want to register to vote.

The bottom line here is: *no one is in charge, so say whatever the hell you want.* No one has any business calling you "Traitor" as if he represented some established gay government whose interests you were required to uphold patriotically. It's been said earlier in this book that we need to develop new ideas about ourselves in order to move forward into a desirable future. But how can we develop new ideas about ourselves if we won't voice them for fear we'll be marked for death by some kind of gay star chamber?

Thomas Jefferson—whose writings on free speech still make for an interesting read—believed that free speech is important because it's the only way to arrive at the truth. Open public debate will, over time, knock down falsehoods and leave the truth standing. He believed that the worst way to serve the truth was to reach final conclusions and then ruthlessly suppress any attempt to challenge them (even if the challenger's ideas are palpably absurd.) This, he said, would lead to the tyranny of the few over the many.

The lack of free debate in the Gay Liberation Movement has led to the unchecked evolution of all kinds of bizarre belief systems. Since no one is allowed to disagree with anybody else without being called a traitor, gay zealots are not required to examine or justify their positions.

The most noticeable of these belief systems to appear in recent years is represented by the ferocious, reactionary political groups that I lump together under the general title of the Anger Movement.

The Anger Movement—populated predominantly, it seems, by enraged young people—is an attempt to take our tired old gay political rhetoric and revitalize it. Underlying this movement is the unconscious realization that we've gone as far as we can with these ideas. The Anger Movers are trying to push those ideas somewhere new, to make them work for us again.

To do this requires three steps:

1 • Invest the old ideas with savage emotion.

2 • Redefine everything, using the most inflammatory language conceivable: the AIDS crisis is the new Black Plague, our legislators' distaste for gay issues is "planned genocide," you and I are "fighting for our lives" in our "war" with the straight world, and

3 • Disregard any social gains we've made over the last twenty-five years. The Anger Movement describes gay people as if we were the illiterate peasant population of a Latin American dictatorship being tortured in concrete bunkers in the jungles, an assertion that contrasts weirdly with the life experience of millions of prosperous, middle-aged, openly-gay men and women who integrated themselves into straight society decades ago.

The public acts of the Anger Movement don't so much involve any kind of planned social program—like lobbying for a gay rights bill—as they do a kind of smug naughtiness—like whamming an archbishop with a custard pie. Anger Movers use the term "queer" instead of "gay" because they know it annoys even other gay people. (I've heard the alternate explanation that to willingly adopt the term "queer" takes away its power as an epithet to be hurled at us by bigots; I am not convinced.) *

One truly irritating characteristic of the Anger Movers is their tendency to lay claim to other people's accomplishments. A band of gay lobbyists will work for years to push

---

* I'm not particularly offended by the term, but given that "queer" means "peculiar" and "gay" means "happy and carefree," I use the latter as my description of choice in the interests of accuracy.

a pro-gay bill through city hall or state congress. On the day before the vote, an Anger group will stage a demonstration in the streets outside. If the vote goes pro-gay, the Anger Movers claim it as their victory, as if their one-day protest had all those government officials quaking in their wingtips.

Anger demonstrations are entertaining; the political process is stupendously boring. And so, because the protest grabs the attention of the press—as lobbying does not—we, too, end up believing that the victory really belongs to the Anger Movers because we never hear about the years of painstaking and tedious work put in by the real heroes, our invisible activists.

There have been several gay anger movements over the past four decades. The explosion of gay civil rights activity that occurred after the Stonewall riots began as an anger movement. But anger movements don't last very long. They either channel themselves into more sober, reflective avenues of expression with multi-leveled and constructive political agendas, or they self-destruct.

Anger is a great motivator. Many of the courageous acts of gay activists in the past were impelled by anger. But anger movements always fall into the trap of thinking that *to be angry is enough.* In truth, anger creates nothing. Anger can, for a time, create the illusion of solidarity; but people who continue to indulge in such negative emotion eventually turn their anger upon each other.

This isn't to suggest that these people should give up their activities. One of the greatest benefits of life in America is freedom of speech, and if these people are angry about something, then they ought to protest any time they want to, even though other gay people don't share their anger or their world view. And it would be wrong to suppose that their naughty public antics do no good at all: the television news eats up that kind of thing, and the Anger Movers serve to keep gay issues on the TV screens of millions of straight households on a regular basis. At election times, politicians sometimes monitor their own public statements so as to avoid embarrassing retaliation from gay anger groups.

But it's intriguing to wonder if the Anger Movement would ever have gotten started if the Gay Liberation Movement had any kind of forum for coherent debate, rather than our present system of shouting at each other from entrenched positions.

The most appalling aspect of the "thought police" approach to liberation is the recent phenomenon of "outing." Certain famous people who are living in the closet have been revealed to be homosexual by certain gay publications. The motive of these journalists, it is asserted, is that the gay community needs role models and, if none are forthcoming, forced conscription is necessary and acceptable.

It should first be noted that no human cause is so good that unwilling victims can be sacrificed to it. Beyond that, consider this: if there is one essential concept that is the basis of the Gay Liberation Movement it is that *a person ought to be able to live the way he wants to without being interfered with by people who disapprove of how he lives.* And yet now we see this phenomenon of gay people turning to other gay people and saying, "We disapprove of how *you* live. You're not living as we think you should. And so now we're going to interfere with *your* life."

A gay person who deprives another gay person of the right to live as he chooses in order to secure for the rest of us the right to live as we choose is just like these people who pop up once in a while who want to protect the American Way of Life by making it illegal to criticize it, blithely ignoring the fact that the right to say whatever you please is the basis of the American Way of Life. Why is it human beings always seem to end up trying to defend their most cherished values by violating them entirely? We fight for peace. We try to preserve freedom by limiting it. We "out" unwilling people to serve the cause of freedom of choice.

———————

Gay people cherish the idea of a gay community because it is an idea of *home*. And home is, as Robert Frost put it, a place where, when you have to go there, they have to take you in. We all want to believe that there is some group of people in our lives to whom we are automatically and permanently connected through bonds of mutuality that cannot be broken by any external circumstance. For many people this means family; but many gay people are estranged from their families. We long for there to be a community of people out there to whom we belong in a manner that cannot be questioned.

But that can never be. Consciousness can only attract similar consciousness. A lonely, disconnected person can only attract other lonely, disconnected people. Someone who has categorized himself as a victim will only attract other victims. Even if there is a gay community out there, you will only have as many people in your life as your consciousness entitles you to have. No more, no less. There may be a community of millions out there, but you will know only as many people as you allow yourself to know. So, the existence or nonexistence of the gay community may be a hot issue for political workers, but for you as an individual it is entirely irrelevant.

Within the Gay Liberation Movement there are many small communities. There's a community of political activists. There's a community of AIDS caregivers. There's a "dance community" of tavern owners, their staffs and their patrons. There's a community of recovering alcoholics and substance abusers. But I believe that most gay men do not fit comfortably under any of these categories. No, not even the dance club category.

And many gay men who don't fit into any of these categories frustrate themselves by trying to fit in. These men feel guilty. They feel there is a gay community out there and that they're lonely because they've failed to contribute to it. So, they attend their first political action meeting only to run screaming from the room with their hair standing on end after the first half hour.

Connections must be built. They must be earned through

love, commitment to people before causes, keeping agreements, patience, generosity and—an unpopular word—duty. You must build your own community of relationships in your own life using the materials you have at hand. Like Bad Neighbor Sam, you'll find that this process connects you with the larger world beyond your daily routine. You build your personal community by living your life well, doing the work necessary to maintain your personal connections and by exercising kind regard towards other people just because they're people, not because they're a certain kind of people.

Before you try to hook up with the gay community, make sure you're a member of the human race.

————————

A few years ago, in a city in which I lived, I called a friend one Sunday and suggested we go to the Gay Pride Festival that was being held that morning.

"The Gay Pride Festival?" he said with some distaste. "Why the hell do you want to do that?"

I was momentarily lost for an answer. "Well, it's the Gay Pride Festival. I'm gay. You're gay. We're proud. Let's go." Besides, I reminded him, several of the organizers were friends of ours.

As if to humor me, he agreed.

No sooner were we there than I realized it wasn't going to be as much fun as I'd anticipated. The festival was set up in a large lot adjacent to the principal gay neighborhoods of that city. Hundreds of people were walking about together in the intense afternoon sunshine.

For a festival, it was not particularly, well, *festive*. There were no rides or games. In a city packed with gay-owned restaurants, there was no food. There were booths with gay-related materials for sale: books, buttons, rainbow flags. My chiropractor had a booth where he was giving complimentary spinal exams. Dour volunteers walked around handing out safe sex kits. (One object contained in mine was a mystery to me. I tried to imagine it attached to various parts of my body until a lesbian acquaintance explained to me, rather coldly, that it was a dental dam.) Most of the booths represented various gay rights and AIDS support organizations whose representatives passed out free literature. On a raised dais dominating the fairground, an angry poet was reading one of his works which was apparently about being a "nigger," though the author was white. He was replaced by a rock band that played what sounded like one deafening, nerve-jarring chord repeated endlessly. The crowd milled around disconsolately, as if none of them were quite sure why they were there. We ran into people we knew. They seemed as dispirited and bewildered as we were.

After half an hour of this, I stopped in my tracks and looked around me. "Can you imagine," I said, "being a young, gay kid just out of the closet, trying to derive a sense of identity and self-worth from *this?* And from bars and bathhouses? Porno videos? Guys with mustaches in drag? Protest marches and AIDS vigils?"

"I take it you've had enough," my friend said.

We left the fairgrounds, walked to where we'd parked his car and got in.

We sat for a moment in silence.

"Why on earth did we do that?" I said.

Solemnly, he placed the key in the ignition and started the car. "I know exactly why we did it," he said.

"Oh? And why is that?"

He pulled out into traffic. "To remind ourselves why we don't live in that consciousness the rest of the year round."

"Aha," I said. "That's it. That is it."

Sorta True Story #5

The Radical Dinner Party

It's a strange fact of life in these United States that religion is the only area of daily living in which people are admired for believing ridiculous things. In all other areas—politics, sexuality, the arts, the environment, the treatment of animals—debate is loud and wide open. But here in a country that has freedom of religion rarely matched by other nations, it's considered the depths of bad taste to express opinions about the spiritual beliefs of other people.

We're expected to admire the capacity for unwavering belief *for its own sake,* even if we think the ideas in question are absurd. "Having faith" is not, to our thinking, a matter of personal certainty which has evolved from personal experience, but simply an emotional and unquestioning attachment to a set of ideas.

I've seen many fascinating dinner table conversations degenerate into sullen silence when the subject of spirituality enters the talk; each person speaks in turn and everybody else politely nods their heads as if in agreement. Even if the beliefs of Person #2 contradict entirely the beliefs of Person #1, everyone behaves as if they were all, in some vague, inarticulate kind of way, saying exactly the same thing, thus rendering any exchange of ideas unnecessary.

I attended a dinner party years ago where most of the guests were political radicals and activists of one left-wing stripe or another. When it was discovered that I was a minister—a fact I resolutely concealed at social gatherings—the talk turned to religion and the round robin of polite head-nodding began.*

One guest explained that his parents' religion involved a vengeful, angry God who kept an eye on our actions and

---

* My career as a minister was brief.

judged our worthiness, and in which salvation was available only through this angry god's son.

"Well, that's a silly kind of idea, isn't it?" I said.

Everyone stared blankly.

"Uh, I mean, the idea that God is like that. I mean, the universe couldn't even *exist* if God was like that."

The temperature in the room dropped measurably. Our host said under his breath to his lover, "He's doing it again."

"I hardly think," said one of the guests coldly, "that we can criticize the religious beliefs of other people."

"Why not?" I replied. "What if their beliefs are dangerous, destructive nonsense? What if their beliefs demean certain kinds of people or disregard the integrity of the planet's biosphere?"

"Well, *nonsense* or not," said the same guest, "it's just where they're at right now."

Everyone nodded in unison and the talk went on.

The group heaved a collective sigh of relief when the circle was completed and we were able to change the subject.

A recent political conflict was mentioned. People became animated. Their eyes lit up. Someone expressed the view that the people who opposed this new political initiative were idiots.

"Well," I said, "I hardly think we can criticize the political beliefs of other people."

The temperature dropped again.

"Oh, sweet Jesus," said our host, apparently returning to our previous topic of conversation.

"What do you *mean*," said the same guest who'd challenged me before, "that we can't criticize? These people are rich, right-wing control addicts."

"Well, control addicts or not," I said smiling, "it's just where they're at right now."

The ensuing discussion was lively.

As a nation we have a kind of schizophrenic approach to religion: on one hand we think the topic is so sacrosanct that it can't be discussed objectively, while on the other hand we think that people's spiritual beliefs aren't very important anyway. I mean, they don't *affect* anything, do they? Politics, we say, that's where people's ideas have an impact.

In truth, the politics of a country are never anything more than an outpicturing of the religious beliefs—that is, the principal life concepts—of the majority of the people. Most of today's political hot potatoes—abortion, prostitution, narcotics availability—are so very heated exactly because they are religious debates disguised as civil rights controversies. And many kinds of activities are illegal not because they can be shown to inflict any real damage on society, but rather because they offend traditional religious morality.

Do Your Mindwork
Part 4: How to Get a Life

We're constantly pressured to become who we aren't, to want what we don't need, to praise what we don't care about. Here's a little checklist that will help you to keep your mental equilibrium and remember who you really are and help you focus your life in a direction that will make you happy, no matter what opinion other people may have of your choices.

1 • Admit what you love

You are Life's way of being you. Humans are designed to be spontaneous. It's your job to express in your activities what Spirit can't express through the automatic workings of nature. Your personal likes and dislikes are not insignificant side issues. You'll produce the highest quality of life for yourself, including the greatest money supply, by involving yourself in what you love, regardless of what other people might think of it and regardless of how impractical it might seem for purposes of generating income.

Make a list of everything that interests you and elicits pleasure in you: beekeeping, mud wrestling, marine biology, golf, collecting ceramic dolls, sculpting with hamburger, defrosting people's refrigerators, whatever. Something on that list is the key to your fortune and your happiness.

2 • Don't be tasteful

One of the basic tenets of the new spirituality is that Life has already given you everything; you need only choose what aspect of that Infinite Gift you wish to experience. And yet, many people are embarrassed to tell Spirit what they really want. They pray (or treat or affirm) for less than what they desire so that God won't think they're greedy. They ask for a "nice relationship" when what they want is a frenzied and shallow affair with an ice skater. They ask for enough money to pay the electric bill while harboring a secret desire to be filthy rich. They treat for good health when what they want is to be young and gorgeous.

The Infinite isn't a Victorian governess who can be put off by frankness and naughty talk. Whatever you want, it's already yours. Go for it. Take, take, take. Pig out. The Infinite is infinite.

3 • Don't expect points for endurance

You don't get cosmic brownie points for suffering graciously. If it hurts, send it away. The Infinite won't reward you later for misery endured today. It's your present personal growth and joyful living that's being affected, not your future. You must choose what is acceptable to you and refuse what is unacceptable. Spirit *will* give and you *will* receive. Tell It what you want or It'll give you something else.

Many good people are put off by this concept. They think this means that the spiritual dimension of life is cold, removed, aloof, that we are living in a kind of automated universe where compassion and freedom are illusions masking some inexorable and inhuman Master Plan.

But look at it this way: If a boy falls from a third story window and is severely injured, we're shocked and saddened. We do not, however, rail in moral outrage against the force of gravity, demanding to know why it couldn't have suspended its operation in just this one case. We can accept that people who go out third story windows are taking their chances.

In an interview, Mae West was asked how she'd maintained her youth and energy into extreme old age.

"Honey," she said, "you got to find out what ages you, and send that bitch away."

4 • Put a little more into life than you take out of it

People ought to spend less time trying to make themselves lovable and devote more time to making themselves useful.

If you will set about doing something because you think it needs to be done, you'll find that many of your supposed personality problems evaporate. To make a contribution to life sweeps away a host of small neuroses. Furthermore, small courtesies and considerations can give you tremendous power over your life experiences. Say "thank you" to the bus driver. Give money to one of those nature groups that send you "junk" mail. Hold the elevator instead of pretending that you can't find the "Door Open" button. Introduce people to each other. Tip generously. Recycle your newspapers. Write to your congressmen. Use environmentally safe cleaning products. Send thank you notes. Don't say, "I will if they will." Say, "I will even if they won't."

Taking every opportunity to add a little to life will have far-reaching and beneficial effects on your relationships, your income, and your health. When Life sees someone who is giving a little bit more than he receives, It brings him opportunities to give more and more, and enlarges his mind and capabilities in order to meet the new demands placed on him.

We grow not by acquiring more but by giving more and thereby forcing Life to express more of Itself through us and around us.

to
Attract Friendship

AFFIRMATION

I am never alone.

There is a Presence that surrounds me, that knows who I am, that seeks to give generously of Itself to me.

This Presence speaks to me through people, because people are one of Its ways of being. I am one of Its ways of being. This Presence tells me about myself through the people It brings into my life.

This Presence thinks I'm wonderful exactly the way I am, and It will bring into my life people who share Its viewpoint, if I will only let them in.

I let them in now. The world is full of people who will love me exactly the way I am. I let them in now.

There's nothing I need to become. There's no changes I need to make. There's no qualifying exam I need to pass in order to have friends.

I have nothing further to learn from painful relationships. I have nothing further to learn from people who expect me to prove myself to them. I have nothing further to learn from people who take without giving.

The world is full of wonderful people who will love me exactly the way I am. I let them in now.

And behind those people, seeing through their eyes and speaking through their mouths, is the Presence of Life Itself, that knows me only as another perfect aspect of what It is.

Chapter Five

This Relationship Ain't Big Enough for Both of Us

Love and the Lovelorn

*One is not superior merely because
he sees the world as odious*
                    —Chateaubriand

People routinely spend their lives in pursuit of love without ever taking a moment's thought as to what love is or why they want it so badly. (We pursue other things with a similar lack of definitions—like youth, success, fulfillment, healing, happiness and security.)

Occasionally we announce that we have "fallen in love," or we wonder if the person we are presently "seeing" (our euphemism for "having sex with") really loves us. The moment at which one partner says "I love you" is always a tense one: will the other say "I love you, too, Michael," or will he just say, "Thank you"?

The desire for love is immensely powerful in us, and we intuitively sense that love is what we need to make all things well in our lives. We notice that doing things we love to do is always easier and more fulfilling than doing what we don't love, and yet we somehow never put together a coherent definition of love for ourselves.

It's far easier to determine what love isn't:

1 • Love is not nagging

Many lovers are dreadful nags. "Comb your hair. What will people think?" "Can't you wear anything nicer than that?" Or, "You were very inattentive to me at that party!"

This isn't love, this is fear of a loss of status. You're afraid that people will think less of you if you're married to a slob, or if your lover ignores you in public.

"No, no! I just want him to be the best he can be!"

You have no right to decide what somebody else's best should consist of, not even if you're married to him. Your lover is old enough to dress himself, and you're old enough to be at a party alone.

2 • Love is not putting up with someone else's vile behavior.

"He's cruel to me, but I still love him."

Why?

It's a profound statement of your own belief in your own worthlessness if you think you must endure personal abuse in order to sustain a relationship. Clearly, you need to develop a better opinion of yourself. Holding on tenaciously to a lover who is making you miserable is a way of saying that you're so undesirable that you fear he'll be your last lover. Or it's a stubborn refusal to admit that you made a mistake getting involved with him in the first place.

Wasting five years on a bad relationship is not a good reason to waste ten.

3 • Love is not expensive.

It's very sad to listen to some older, wealthy gay man waxing sentimental over the deep and abiding love of his twenty-two-year-old boyfriend—for whom, by the way, he has just purchased a condo, a sports car, a Lhasa apso, and the entire Perry Ellis fall line. This isn't love, it's a business arrangement. The older gentleman has purchased the rights to the younger man's ass.

There is nothing—nothing *at all*—wrong with a business arrangement. It can be a lot of fun and very rewarding to both parties involved.

Let's just not call it "love."

4 • Love is not an emotion.

Emotions are transient reactions to outward events, and the belief that love is an emotion rises from the conception of love as an influence that descends upon us from the outside, just as the phrase "falling in love" indicates the belief in the randomness of finding a mate, the right-place-at-the-right-time school of thought that regards any meeting of true lovers to be merely a happy accident.

Love isn't a reaction to accidentally stumbling upon Mr. Right. Love is a causative agent of change and growth that proceeds from within the self. Love is not the product of a happy confluence of circumstances, it's a spiritual energy, emanating from the individual, that draws to him all that is like himself.

No one will ever come into your life and fill it with love. Only you will ever be able to do that for yourself. If there's a lack of love in your life, it's because there's a lack of love in you. Many of us intuitively sense that the sterility of our personal lives is our own individual responsibility, and yet on a rational level we can't figure out how this can be so. This produces confusion, irritation, and ultimately bitterness toward a world that seemingly refuses to cough up what we so desperately need while giving it in great abundance to other people.

What to do about this sorry state leads us to the question of what love is.

If I needed to answer that question only for myself, I would simply say, "Love is God." This definition satisfies me. Or I might say "Love is Growth" or "Love is Peace of Mind" or "Love is Security," because God and Love and Growth and Peace and Security are all synonymous, at least they are in my neighborhood. `

That isn't a definition that many people will find useful. In fact, it's an abstract definition that many of the people who read this book won't want to deal with at all. That's fine. Nobody's saying they have to.

It will be far more instructive to deal with love in its active phase in our experience.

Try this on for size: *Love is your relationship with whatever you think you can't live without.*

Look and see what peculiar loves we have. We love jobs that exhaust us and grind us down; we wouldn't leave them for the world. We love angry, combative, and frequently violent living situations. We love poverty. And we love *boredom.*

This is a far cry from our usual conception of love as that heart-fluttering rush experienced when sighting Mr. Right across a crowded room. Nor is it the usual exercise in positive thinking that tells us that if we're consistently nice to people they'll be nice in return.

Certainly no adult needs to be told that if we are persistently pleasant to everyone we'll receive a far higher percentage of pleasant responses. That's simple common sense, and it's kid stuff. Anybody past the age of ten knows to do this. (Whether or not they practice it is another story.)

We're talking about love as a causative agent, a spiritual power that produces and maintains the quality and the particulars of our outer experience, and that is the motive force behind any improvements we may wish to make in our lives. This spiritual power responds to our beliefs and instantly sets about demonstrating them in our outer experience. To produce a life filled with love, we must change our beliefs *about* love.

We must let go of our destructive loves—the need for grindingly hard work, the scarcity of money, the inevitability of disease—and turn our focus onto our good loves—our inborn right to live as we wish, our natural need to be rich, our intended freedom from illness. We must give this Infinite Loving Power something new to work with in us.

^{Do}Your **Mindwork**
Part 5: Love Takes Practice

1 • Stop thinking of love as something outside of you.

Stop thinking of it as a commodity that can be acquired. This realization will instantly relax you, because it frees you from so much frantic *needing*. It frees you from desperate searching at the bars, from resenting people who you believe are withholding your happiness from you, from anger directed at an apparently indifferent world. You know now that what you are seeking is within you.

2 • Stop resenting happy people for being happy.

It's no crime. Never take offense at seeing qualities in other people's lives that you wish to see in your own. Don't resent lovers for being in love ("They don't look so happy to *me* !"). Don't resent rich people for being rich ("All rich people are crooks; I'm broke because I'm honest!"). Don't resent creative people for being successful ("I can do that just as well as he can, but I never got the breaks!"). And don't resent healthy, beautiful people for being attractive ("If he works on his body that much, he's either stupid or narcissistic or both!").

When you see anything you consider to be good, praise it mentally. Beautiful bodies, popularity, wealth, artistic fulfillment, *praise it*. It feels good.

3 • Learn to practice forgiveness.

Never try to assign blame. Proving to yourself that somebody else is causing a problem for you is not only spiritually inaccurate, it has no effect whatsoever on the problem.

Whenever someone gives you grief, instead of getting enraged, tell yourself, "I forgive this person for acting like a jerk, and I forgive myself for getting angry about it."

Forgiveness is simple for many people once they're given the technique. For others of us, it's like digging ditches. We're in no hurry to give up a grudge. Sometimes a person's thinking has to become an endless litany of forgiveness as he forgives and forgives one person after another, and always himself as well. It can be lot of work.

4 • Get your old dreams down off the shelf.

The fantasies you entertain about how you would like to live aren't fantasies at all. They're the Infinite's messages to you; they're the images of what happiness is to you.

Do you want to be rich? Then decide it's possible and start mulling over ideas of how to make it so for you.

Do you have creative longings that you've been ignoring? Get to work on one of them. It will take you places you weren't expecting to go. Nice places.

Do you wish you had a beautiful body? Well, what's stopping you? Think out a way to improve your physical appearance and set yourself lovingly to that program. (If it's painful and boring, you're doing it wrong.)

Remember, finding a lover isn't a matter of being in the right place at the right time; it's a matter of being the right person all the time.

Stop looking for love and start living your life lovingly. Stop looking for Mr. Right and set about becoming Mr. Right.

A Majority of One

Most ironically, many gay men of my acquaintance fear that they can improve themselves *too much*, that they can become so involved with their own interests that no one will ever come along with whom they can be compatible. They're afraid of being unique.

The thinking here seems to be that your chances of hooking a husband are better if you can appeal to the widest spectrum of people possible. So, generic is good, unusual is bad.

"There aren't a lot of men like the kind I'm looking for," they say.

Well, are you looking for a lot of them? Most of us only want one. You don't have to test-drive fifty possible candidates before making a decision, you know.

Your greatest happiness lies in what is unique about you. *Be extraordinary.* If you truly involve yourself in all that you love, you'll be surrounded by people of like consciousness, of like loves. You'll never need to go prospecting at the bars again. You'll find loving people everywhere that you are.

The wonderful man you've been searching for is *you.* Become him, and he'll stay with you forever.

You're the only person who can never leave you. Make sure you're good company for yourself.

Love is what you feel toward whatever you think you can't live without.

What are your loves?

Sorta True Story #6

Lovelorn George

George is a forty-year-old gay man who desires a relationship with a significant other. He's been investigating his spirituality for a few years and he's done a lot of self-examination. He's very clear on the fact that the "type" of people that he seeks out for casual sex—specifically, skinny, good-looking blond men in their early twenties who George calls "twinkies"*—are not suitable as a marriage prospects. He's compiled a "laundry list" of characteristics that he will require in a viable spouse; he knows what he wants.

George will perform daily spiritual work to demonstrate such an individual in his life. But even before he begins his daily work, at the moment his "laundry list" was finished, the moment his desire was clear in his mind, the Infinite immediately selected several suitable candidates who satisfied all the items on George's list.† Since the Infinite contains everything and everyone within Itself, It had no trouble in locating these men. It instantly connected them in consciousness to George. It then began to create events around George and these candidates that would bring them together with each other at fortuitous times.

A friend of Candidate #1 is planning a party. He gets the notion to invite his friend Brian, who is a passing acquaintance of George's. George gets the notion to try a new restaurant in his neighborhood. On the same day, Brian gets the same notion. They run into each other at lunch. In the course of conversation, Brian spontaneously invites George to be his guest at the upcoming party. George isn't remotely

---

* Cheap, sweet, quickly dispatched and entirely non-nutritional.

† The standard romantic ideal is that each of us has one special someone out there somewhere. Actually, any individual has a multitude of suitable marriage prospects.

interested in Brian as a marriage prospect, but he's a spiritual student doing daily affirmation, so he knows better than to turn down a surprise invitation.

As they arrive at the party, George catches sight of another of his "types," (blond twinkies) and decides he would like to make contact, even though he decided earlier that he needed to stop indulging this tiresome hormonal impulse and to meet a more mature man. As a result, when he is introduced to Candidate #1, George's mind is already focused on the possibility of a sexual encounter with the blond twinkie, and so he pays no attention to Candidate #1. The opportunity for this relationship is lost. Candidate #1 thinks George is attractive initially, but he sees that George is a "twinkie-chaser" and so lowers his opinion of him.

The blond turns George down and the evening is a total loss.

The Infinite, which misses nothing, registers and records George's rejection of Candidate #1. The movement of consciousness which George originally set in motion is canceled.

The next morning, George, more determined than ever, affirms again for his right relationship. We might imagine the Infinite saying, "Huh? Say *what?* I thought we let that one go! Oh, well, all right..." And all those abandoned connections are plugged in again.

Complicating all this are George's transparent negatives: one is that he thinks being gay is inferior to being straight. He's been out of the closet for years, quite sexually active and quite vocal about his lifestyle. He says he's proud to be gay, and he is. And yet, attaching itself to every one of George's gay-related thoughts is the transparent negative that gayness is a fallen state; he tends to see other gay people as living in a moral vacuum, as not being as acute and introspective as himself, as being insecure and hypercritical. And below that transparent negative is another, the idea that sex of any kind tends to cheapen the participants. (Almost everybody gets taught this one.)

So when Candidate #2 flirts with George in the checkout line at the grocery store, George rules him out as a possibility. "I'm certainly not interested in someone who cruises in grocery stores," he tells himself.

Of course, George cruises in grocery stores all the time.

Candidate #3 gets a little farther. They meet at the dry cleaners and #3 asks George to go out with him. They date several times. It's great. They go to bed together several times. It's great.

But George blows it. Another of his transparent negatives is that "time is running out." George is 40. He's never had a long-term relationship. This hardly surprises *us,* but it's a complete mystery to him: he's reasonably good-looking, talented, solvent, personable. But whenever a new beau shows promise, as with Candidate #3, George is ready to call the real estate agent and buy a love cottage after the first week. Although he wisely hides this impulse from his boyfriends, they detect it anyway and they eventually flee.

And so does Candidate #3.

The next day, George treats again for a right relationship, and the Infinite continues the candidacy process.

Fortunately, the Infinite can't get exasperated with George and just kill him.

And so we say good-bye to the spectacle of Lovelorn George, who is presented almost daily with viable lovers and who either turns them down or fails to recognize them for what they are. He may well go on doing this for another ten years, after which he'll decide that he's "too old" for love and he'll retire into bitterness and the occasional prostitute.

What's that you say?

You want a happy ending?

Very well: here it is...

George has been a spiritual seeker for a while, and he admits to himself—reluctantly—that his failure to demonstrate a significant other can't be blamed on Spirit. The Infinite doesn't ever fail and he knows that. He knows he's failing himself somehow.

He begins a new program: he *gives up* the idea of finding a lover and instead affirms daily for mental clarity about himself and his inability to find a life partner.

In the course of the next several months, he experiences several revelations regarding his negative attitude towards gayness. And he at last stops pretending that he's not afraid of getting old. This doesn't magically change his belief system overnight, but he does become aware of his transparent negatives and learns to manage them through his understanding of Truth.

He decides to participate, as an exercise in generosity, in a local volunteer program of radio reading for the blind. No one knows he's doing this. He doesn't get paid for his time. He just thinks it's a nice thing to do.

He works alongside a nice man who runs the small broadcasting studio. After a month, George is astonished when this studio manager asks him out on a date. George is further astonished by how many items on his "laundry list" this man fulfills.

They make it work.

And there's your happy, and entirely plausible, ending.

^{Do} ^{Your} **Mindwork**

Part 6: How to Prepare for the Arrival of Mr. Right

1 • Resolve your relationship with your parents.

Ah, you weren't expecting that one, were you? You've been keeping the parent thing on a back burner.

Your parents were your first relationship, and that relationship will color all your subsequent relationships. Your parents are the source of all your basic belief systems about life and what to expect from it. If you don't confront the issues in your family relationships and resolve them, then you'll recreate them in any intimate relationship you enter into.

This isn't to say that you need to go back to your parents and drag them into therapy with you. Many parents are not amenable to that. Remember, your parents don't know you need to forgive them; they think you need to *apologize* to them. You might have to do the work by yourself in the privacy of your own mind. But do it. Before you try to be married to someone.

And never pair up with someone who's mad at his mommy.

2 • Get a Life

You're going to have a tough time sharing your life with somebody if your life already bores the hell out of *you*. You must attract a lover with the quality and content of your life, not with the size of your pecs.

3 • Stop Seeking Novelty

Our entertainment media inundates us with stories about wildly mismatched people who meet under bizarre circumstances and establish a relationship in which their eccentricities perfectly balance each other out. This may make for good dramatic tension in telling a story, but it's not how real relationships work. Certainly there are successful relationships between people who, on the surface, seem to be wildly mismatched. But chances are you'll end up with someone who's just like you.

And if that prospect bores you, you might want to take another look at your attitude towards yourself.

4 • Don't plan to change him.

A disastrous strategy in which many gay men indulge is to select a dreadfully inappropriate lover with the idea in mind of putting that person through a process of renovation that will turn him into the right person. A Rhodes scholar will go after some sarcastic, addictive, black-clad creature of the night while assuring himself, "Oh, he only needs a little love." A man of mature years will select a pretty young blond for a lover, thinking that blondie will "benefit from my years of experience." The plan is to get someone young and *train* him to be the right person. This is predicated on the laughable assumption that the older guy will be running the relationship. And it can lead to the rather pathetic spectacle of a multi-million-dollar corporation being run by a nineteen-year-old gymnast.

It's impractical and also deceitful to enter into a relationship with a person with the intent of turning him into someone else. You must want him for who he is and he must want you for who you are. How would you feel starting a relationship with someone if you knew he planned on turning *you* into someone he found acceptable?

5 • Don't Hurry

It will take as long as it takes.

A client who was doggedly doing spiritual mind treatments, visualizations and who-knew-what-else to manifest a right relationship for himself kept asking me *when, WHEN, WHEN!* "How long will it take, Greg?" he'd say. "You tell me that all manifestation is instantaneous! When does it happen! When do I meet him?"

"I don't know," I said. "Suppose it took five years?"

"Five years!" he said. "Five years! Do you know how old I'll be in five years! I'll be forty-four, Greg! Forty-four years old! I can't go that long without a lover! I need my lover right now!"

I shrugged. "How old will you be in five years if you *do* get a lover?"

6 • Make sure you're already getting lots of sex.

If your ethics permit, of course. It's important to be sexually satisfied before you decide to embark on a relationship with somebody. If you're not, then your hormones will choose your mate for you, and your hormones aren't as smart as you are. Hormones are terrible judges of character.

Too many people go into relationships for purposes of convenient, ongoing sexual gratification. Once that gratification is complete—and it doesn't take very long at all—the couple discovers that they find each other rather boring. Most therapists will tell you that the sexual part of a relationship is over after the first year. Two years, tops. Couples may go on having sex after that, but only if they can maintain interest in each other in other areas of their married life.

The best way to make sure that you're not getting married just for the sex is to make it unnecessary to do so; make sure your sex life is already healthy and satisfying before you choose with whom to commit.

AFFIRMATION

for
Self - Worth

There is only one Mind, one Power, one Infinite Love operating throughout this universe. This Infinite Loving Power is operating within me right now. This Power desires nothing other than to express all of Its qualities through me, as me. This is my desire as well, so this omnipotent Mind and I are in perfect accord.

This Perfect Intelligence is the guiding force in my mind, and It always sees to it that I know what is best for me.

I do not embrace that which destroys me. I now release and reject any conditions in my experience that do not please me, whether it be financial lack, ill health, loneliness, or frustration.

I have nothing further to learn from negative experiences.

The Omnipresent Mind supports me in all ways, enlightens me from within, enfolds me and protects me. It points me on my way, and I always have the good sense to heed Its advice.

I am grateful for Its good care and I joyfully release myself into It now, knowing that It has all my best interests at heart.

Part Two

Deathbed Groupies

It proves what they say, give the public what they want to see and they'll come out for it.
> —*Red Skelton at the well-attended funeral of movie producer Harry Cohn*

I ask those who urge me to take medications to wait at least until I have regained enough strength to enable me to stand the effort and the risk.
> —*Montaigne*

Chapter Six

The Joy of AIDS
How We Think About It

*A man who reads nothing at all is better educated
than a man who reads nothing but newspapers.*
        —Thomas Jefferson

Everybody loves AIDS.

AIDS is the greatest. We are crazy about it. We can't
stop talking about it. It's on our minds every time we sit on
a toilet, drink out of somebody else's glass, or kiss our
mothers. It's gay America's number-one topic for dinner
table conversation; it beats the weather hands down.

The only people who don't love AIDS are the people
who have it. I guess being sick makes you grouchy.

But that's okay, because we love people who have
AIDS. They're our heroes. They get to go on television.
Everybody turns out for the funeral.

In earlier pages, we've put forward the idea that all
physical conditions proceed from belief systems. If this is so,
surely AIDS is the product of an upbringing that has taught
us that, as homosexuals, we have no proper place in this
world. We've been convinced, at some level of our consciousness, that we have less right to be here than other
people have.

A disease that takes away your ability to fight disease is
a truly perverse notion, something that a particularly wicked

91

science fiction writer might cook up. That we've managed to inflict this upon ourselves is incredible.

Phrases like "inflicted this upon ourselves" can start a fist-fight. The idea that people are responsible for their own misfortunes is a sensitive issue, especially in the matter of disease. People don't like to hear it, and we have a natural instinct to protect those who are sick or in trouble.

We don't need to beat the concept to death right here. But try this on for size: there's an automatic process in this Universe—let's call it the Law—that converts belief into experience. *Thought takes form.* That's the Law. How you imagine this process working is your own business. But sooner or later, anyone who wants to succeed at anything must make peace with the idea that what he experiences in life is an inevitable outpicturing of the way he believes.

Anyone can accept this if he keeps it at the level of mere positive thinking, i.e., if you adopt a positive attitude, life will be easier for you. That's true enough. But people who experiment with this process by which belief becomes experience find that the experiences they produce often occur without any hands-on participation on their part and often take the form of medically inexplicable healings or of strings of coincidences that fly in the face of the law of probability. There are strong indications that there is an active Power at work in these instances that operates beyond the individual's personal sphere of influence.

The mental process by which we unknowingly created this illness for ourselves is the same mental process by which we can consciously regain our health. Life always gives us that to which our beliefs entitle us.* Change the belief and the experience changes equivalently. As was said by Ernest Holmes, the author of *the Science of Mind,* "The thing that makes you sick is the thing that makes you well."

---

*Perhaps it's worth noting here that prior to the discovery of penicillin in the early 1940s, all sexually transmitted diseases were generally incurable and often fatal, and had been so throughout human history. It's only in the last fifty years that sex has been possible without fear of death. AIDS isn't a new problem, it's a new version of a very old problem.

People with AIDS need, first and foremost, to change their thinking about Life and their relationship to it. They need to realize that they have Life's permission to live.

If that sounds simplistic to you—too easy to be true— then you've never tried it. A person with AIDS is presented every day with powerful inducements to remain sick. His doctors—who he's been taught to believe have the last word in such matters—tell him that there is little hope. His own body produces dreadful symptoms. And, most deadly of all, he is *rewarded for being sick* by being surrounded by a coterie of loving admirers. People who never gave a damn about him when he was well are suddenly falling all over him with concern now that he's dying.

Let's not accuse all these helpful people of being ghoulish. Of course, in nursing the sick, they're operating from their highest ideals of conduct. I know many people who've taken it upon themselves to care for those dying of AIDS, and their work is profoundly fulfilling to them.

But there is an alternative to helping people to die with dignity.

You can help them to live.

I believe that the principal reason we rally so fervently around people with AIDS is that *it feels good to be able to care for someone at last.* With gay life as it is, filled with so much loneliness and frustration, it's a relief to finally happen upon someone who can't get along without our support.

Many people thought that the AIDS epidemic would be the thing that would finally *force* us to become a community. Surely, they thought, those bar-hopping, hedonistic queens out there will finally have to get serious about liberation and life and solidarity. And, certainly, AIDS has thrown a damper on the party atmosphere that characterized the 1970s and has served to motivate many people into political action. But the fear of death and the onslaught of the disease symptoms have in many cases isolated us from each other more than ever.

People with AIDS need our love, but not our sympathy. We must help them to live well, not to die gracefully. When we lavish affection on a disease sufferer, we give him this message: "We love you because you are sick." The logical extension of this idea—which the sufferer's mind will automatically make—is, "The sicker I get, the more they will love me. And if I die, there will be no end of praise for me."

Ethically, it's our responsibility to sympathize with the sick. Spiritually, however, it's our duty to refuse to accept the power of the illness; that's something we can't do while in a sympathetic state of mind.

And, as for this disease sufferer needing your love, didn't he always need your love? Why wait until someone is on his deathbed to love him? If we were to show each other, on a daily basis, just a fraction of the love we lavish on people with AIDS, perhaps there would be no people with AIDS.

————

When I suggest denying the power of the illness, I don't mean physical action. Please don't go to your poor friend who is languishing with pneumocystis pneumonia, drag him out of bed, shove his running clothes against his chest, and say "All right, Randy! Enough of this AIDS nonsense! Twenty laps!"

Please don't.

Consider this:

My friend Mark heard that his friend James in L.A. had AIDS. Mark is not a particularly committed metaphysician, but he's accepted the idea that all disease begins with a belief. He determined to fly out to see James and sell him on the idea of seeing a spiritual practitioner.

Before he left, I told him: "Make sure James understands that your visit is not a reward to him for being sick. Make it clear to him that you are there to support him in his healing, not to hold his hand in the face of the inevitable."

Mark did just that. However, as things turned out, James could not have been less interested in spiritual healing. He came from a family of doctors and had "done time in med school," as he put it. He had a firm belief in the finality of medical knowledge.

Mark found himself in a bizarre situation. James and his sympathetic friends would sit around and sigh and say profound things like "We're hoping for a miracle." When Mark would suggest that James get himself to a metaphysical practitioner and get to work on his own miracle, *it was as if they could not hear what he was saying.* His consciousness was so at odds with that of his companions that his statements failed to make any impression on their conscious minds at all.

This hasn't slowed Mark down one bit. Whenever he is with James, and whenever he thinks of James, he always sees him as whole, healthy, and full of energy. He has refused, in his mind, to accept the power of the disease. Ever.

And something very interesting has happened: James is supposed to have died by now.

He's fine.

He's started a new business, and it's flourishing. He has as much energy as he's ever had. He has a boyfriend. He's not suffering *any* symptoms. His life is going on pretty much the way it did before he got AIDS.

James inwardly wanted to be well, and Mark, inwardly, refused to see him as anything but. Spirit has responded to the combination of James's desire and Mark's faith.

James doesn't know it yet, but he's healed.

Mark knows it. Mark never knew anything but.*

Unknown Man Has Nice Day! Details at Eleven!

The news media love AIDS better than anything. AIDS is boffo box office. For an industry that thrives on conflict and tragedy, AIDS is a godsend. Every AIDS sufferer is automatically a heartstring-tugging human interest story guaranteed to jack up the 11:00 p.m. ratings.

We're bombarded with news about AIDS from every conceivable source: TV, newspapers, magazines, movies,

---

* Since this passage was written, James's doctors have declared him to be in remission. I think that is truly wonderful.

you name it. Science magazines report on the medical aspects, news magazines and TV shows give us death tolls and projected rates of increase, and movie magazines are still finding new angles to play about poor Rock Hudson and any other celebrity who is afflicted. Even sports magazines have managed to get into the act: a recent issue of a national bodybuilding periodical ran an article on how to avoid getting AIDS at the gym. (Say *what* now?). And on the shelves of the gay section of our local book store we can now find AIDS novels, AIDS memoirs, anthologies of AIDS short stories, even books of AIDS poetry; the book jackets inevitably make some reference to "life in the Age of AIDS."

Gay periodicals are particularly given to this. In some gay magazines nearly every article involves AIDS in some way. Even the entertainment section tells us what TV shows will be dealing with AIDS, which Broadway plays, which movies. You'd have thought the only thing of interest Gays were doing these days was contracting lethal illnesses.[*]

The message from the media is simply this:

YOU AREN'T TERRIFIED ENOUGH YET!

Apparently, until we're all running through the streets screaming hysterically and tearing our hair out from fear of AIDS and throwing ourselves out of skyscraper windows in droves every lunch hour from fear of AIDS, the publishing and broadcasting industries will not let up.[†]

We need to keep in mind that newspapers and magazines are periodicals. They must publish at regular intervals in order to survive. This means that they have a certain number of pages they must fill regularly, even when they

---

[*] Actually, if you check out the fiction selection in any gay bookstore you'll find that gay men are doing three interesting things, which are 1) dying of AIDS, 2) coming out of the closet with exquisite poignancy and 3) solving murders.

[†] The irony is that fear was the principle tactic used in the early part of the AIDS crisis to shock people into taking seriously the possibility of infection. Now that everyone is scared out of their wits, the same people who worked so hard to strike fear into the public are working just as hard to contain those fears to prevent hysterical citizens from enacting punitive AIDS legislation.

don't have much in particular to fill them with. So, when they have nothing to tell us about, they must give us something to worry about instead.

Anxiety sells. "This new legislation might seriously effect social security benefits."

It *might* ?

Let's not brand all journalists and their editors as fear mongers. They're bright, businesslike professionals who know what their audience wants. It's not their job to decide for us what we want to read; it's their job to supply our demand, and that's exactly what they do.

I've always thought the idea wrong-headed that the media are responsible for educating us properly. (One tries not to be too grimly amused by parents who are outraged that television is not doing a better job of raising their children.) It's a TV news staff's job to get the highest rating possible. It's a magazine editor's job to keep his magazine in print.

It's our job, as individuals, to listen to the ideas presented by the media and to accept them or reject them intelligently and as we please. Certainly we have the same responsibility as regards the information we're fed about the AIDS crisis. A little intelligent cynicism will keep us mentally healthy.

Until recently, the various AIDS support groups did little to engender a healing consciousness in their members. The well-intentioned volunteers shared the same sense of hopelessness as the people who had the disease. "Meetings" involved little more than glum pronouncements of the spread of the disease and other statistics from the facilitators and expressions of rage from the participants. Some of these facilitators seem to believe that those afflicted will feel better if they can be assured that many other people are dying right along with them.

However, and contrary to common belief, misery doesn't love company.

Given that AIDS is the product of negative mental patterns, the practice of herding its victims together into a room at regular intervals to impress them with the growing destructive power of the illness is the most disastrous course of action possible.

But the situation is changing. People, it seems, are not dying on schedule. Many gays are successfully utilizing mental techniques to achieve their healings, either by working with a practitioner of some kind or through intuitive discoveries of their own methods. The AIDS support groups, to their credit, are growing very curious indeed about all this. Some of them have begun metaphysical healing programs.

The various systems of metaphysical healing are not in competition with medical science. Most practitioners of these systems simply want people to be healed. Not "Healed my way," but just healed, period. They are believers in whatever truly works.

When a doctor tells you a disease is incurable, he's simply saying that he knows no way to help you. No doctor really thinks that AIDS or any disease is literally incurable; otherwise, no cure would be sought. Never accept a doctor's diagnosis as a death sentence. He didn't give you your life and he can't take it away from you. He's just saying that he can't help you. Don't go to your grave because he said you're supposed to.

There's really no reason to be *that* polite to your physician.

Part 7: How to Handle Fear

Fear happens to us all the time, about all sorts of things. Most of these things are nothing to be afraid of. Here's how to deal with a fear you can't shake.

1 • Shutup

Stop yakking about it. In particular, stop talking about what you fear with people who do nothing but morbidly commiserate with you. Talk about it with someone who'll encourage you to deal with it.

And stop talking to *yourself* about it. Fearful thoughts can arise constantly and repeatedly for days, even weeks, at a time. These moments are excellent opportunities to discipline your mind. When that frightening vision turns up in your head once more, say to yourself, *Think about something else!* And then force yourself to contemplate something that pleases you. If you'll do this in a committed way, you'll find that the fear fades away, or at least resurfaces with far less frequency.

2 • Say to yourself, "This moment is it"

You're here. It's now. Is anything happening? Is anything bad happening to you right now? Probably not. You're probably just sitting there scaring yourself half to death. Cut it out. Acknowledge where you are and what's actually happening. Don't suffer from misery that hasn't been inflicted on you. 100% of Spirit is in the room with you right now, and It couldn't are less about this judgment you've pronounced on yourself; It thinks you're wonderful.

3 • Say to yourself, "What's the worst that can happen?"

You owe money on your credit cards and you're worried about it. What's the worst that can happen? Will they send

Gestapo agents over to knock you around? Will you be dragged through the streets and pelted with rocks? Get a grip. What's the worst thing that can happen? A blot on your credit rating, perhaps.

You're involved in a lawsuit? What's the worst that can happen?

You'll lose.

You think your lover is cheating on you? What's the worst that can happen?

It'll turn out to be true.

You think your boss is going to fire you? What the worst that can happen?

He will.

None of these conditions are fatal, or even disfiguring. Calm down. Too often we fail to take action on a problem because we've blown it so out of proportion that we can't bear even to think about it. We're paralyzed by self-generated fear.

If you'll really grit your teeth and visualize the worst, in most cases you'll see that, even in a worst-case scenario, you'll be all right.

4 • Ask yourself, "How responsible am I?"

You know the answer to that one: you're 100% responsible for anything that happens to you. The problem that's scaring you is a manifestation of something in your consciousness and is entirely within your power to change.

This is what people fail to understand who are offended by the idea that a person is 100% responsible for his own problems. If you *aren't* 100% responsible for your problems, that means that external factors have power over you. But if your problem is a reflection of something in your consciousness, if the external factors are merely appliances through which Life shows us what we think, then you have the power to eliminate the problem by changing the consciousness of which it is a reflection. 100% responsibility for what happens to you means 100% power and 100% freedom. It's not bad news; it's the ultimate good news.

When you accept full responsibility for a frightening situation, you give up the considerable pleasure of blaming other people. This is good. Not only is it spiritually inaccurate to blame someone else's consciousness for your problem, but when you blame someone else you lose your power to do anything about what's happening. In response to your assignment of blame, Spirit invests power in whatever person or thing you've designated as the cause of your problem.

Designate the cause as being something inside you, and the solution will be something inside you as well. When you realize that the other guy isn't responsible for your problem, you also realize that there's no reason to fear him.

5 • Ask yourself, "What am I believing?"

At the bottom of every fear is an absurd belief. Usually it's the belief that external things have independent power over you. Alternatively, it's the belief that your situation is beyond Spirit's power to change. "I'll become a homeless person and sell matches in the snow." "Nobody else will ever love me and I'll die alone fifty years from now." "Love is hard to find." "God is punishing me." "Some things aren't meant to be." If you dig up that belief and bring it into the light of spiritual Truth, it'll crumble into dust in your hands.

6 • Ask yourself, "What are my options?"

Chances are there's a simple and viable solution staring you in the face. We get so wrapped up in our fears and so convinced of our own helplessness that we fail to see the opportunities that Life is handing us. Always remember that in this universe every problem carries within itself the seeds of its own destruction.

Make a list of your options. A solution you've never thought of before will present itself while you're writing your list.

to
Heal Fear

Like everything else,
I am made of Spirit.

The thing I fear is also Spirit. The thing I fear is made out of what I am made out of and it expresses the same Divine Presence that I express.

Spirit can never be at odds with Itself. It is never in conflict. Therefore, I can't be in conflict with any part of It, since to stand in opposition to any part of Spirit is to be at odds with myself.

I now set aside my belief in this situation. I turn this over to Spirit and let It resolve this fearful relationship that is within Itself. I am done holding up my end of this conflict.

I no longer participate in this. I let Spirit take up my part of It and resolve everything.

My fear is pointless, because everything is Spirit acting upon Itself. There is nothing to fear in Spirit's universe. I am free right now to live as I choose, and to make such plans as I will.

Chapter Seven

Wallflower at the Danse Macabre

How the Well Can Deal with the Sick

I am so terrified of being bored.
—Marie Antoinette

Since you and I are routinely bombarded by chilling medical statistics, it's sometimes useful to look at the opposite side of the numbers. The next time you hear the latest data about how many people are expected to be HIV-positive by a certain date in the United States, make a note of it. Then check with some sexuality survey that estimates how many gay men there are in the United States. If you contrast the two numbers, you'll find that a whole lot of gay men are expected *not* to have the AIDS virus.

This isn't to minimize the proportions of the epidemic. The number of infected people is tremendous. And the speed at which the disease is spreading is appalling. But we do want to keep it in clear perspective. This isn't the end of gay people. We're not all going to get AIDS and die. Neither is it a "plague," as many writers are fond of calling it. Anyone who thinks AIDS is the new Black Plague ought to read up a little on the old Black Plague and what it did to the population of Europe.

However, AIDS has entered the lives of most gay people. It's hard to find a gay man who doesn't know someone who has it or who's died of it. So it would seem that a lot of healthy gay men are going to have to be around friends who are dying.

Taking care of someone who's dying can be even more painful than dying is. During this medical crisis the well people are going to need just as much support and guidance as those who are ill.

The Myth of Immunity

Your immune system, like all of your body's systems and desires, is a physical outpicturing of spiritual values. Your immune system is a material representation of your divine right to live in harmony with the world. It's the monitoring system that sees to it that you're unmolested by the microorganisms that come your way. It is spiritual Harmony in action.

When this system breaks down, it indicates a fundamental breakdown of good ideas. A belief has been embraced in the sufferer's mind, a belief that the world is inimical to him, that he has no proper place in it.

Many of us are trying to angle our way around spiritual Law by engaging in "safe sex" techniques. The reasoning here is that one can't acquire AIDS if the proper conditions for contagion are avoided.

That's true, certainly. Realize, however, that the negative patterns that produce AIDS in others may still be operating in you, and the Law dictates that all beliefs must manifest eventually. You may avoid getting AIDS by having only safe sex, but those ugly mental patterns must surely manifest something equally dreadful for you at last, either in your body or in your outer experience. *There is no element of chance.*

Let's be very clear about this. In the original edition of this book, my remarks on safe sex were the most wildly misinterpreted.

I'm not comfortable with the recent practice of connecting particular diseases with particular mental conflicts: a bad back means fear of poverty, a case of warts means that you hate your job, arthritis means a fear of moving forward, and so forth; all that strikes me as terribly clever, terrible literary and highly suspect. I believe two different people can manifest the same disease for different reasons. But given that all experience is a reflection of consciousness, it's reasonable to say that any terminal disease must be a manifestation of *Terminal Consciousness.*

Terminal Consciousness isn't suicidal consciousness. It isn't a "death wish" or a desire to die. It isn't even a despairing or sad consciousness necessarily.

Terminal Consciousness is the inability or refusal to have faith in your own future. Terminal Consciousness is the belief that your future is somewhere that you don't need to go or don't want to go. *It is an inability to come up with a good reason to stick around.*

This needn't be a tragic experience. Happy people die, too. A person who has lived out his life with loving relationships, satisfying work, a reasonable regularity of income and a well-working body can come to perceive the future as time better spent elsewhere. If Terminal Consciousness was a mentality of despair, then cheerful people would live forever. But everybody enters Terminal Consciousness sooner or later. Everybody dies.

Many gay men are unable to see the future as a desirable place to live. They see it as a dreary continuation of their past. If we look around ourselves at the quality of life we offer each other in the gay world, it's not a surprise that gay men could enter into Terminal Consciousness.

Where this applies in the matter of safe sex is this: when a person enters into Terminal Consciousness, the Law of Life will make use of whatever is at hand to free him from this world. Heart attacks are the exit-of-choice in this century and cancer is extremely common.* If the AIDS virus is present in the individual, then AIDS will be the tool that the Universe uses to get him out of here.

---

* I never encounter gay men who are chronically worried about getting cancer or having a heart attack. Do you know any?

In other words: *Safe sex will only protect you from AIDS.* If you are a person in Terminal Consciousness, safe sex won't protect you from death. The Infinite will simply have to find some other means by which to manifest your consciousness. If you are in Terminal Consciousness, death is inevitable, even if you scrupulously avoid the AIDS virus. *There is no element of chance.* Some people seem to think that if they can avoid getting AIDS they'll live forever.

Does this mean that if you're not in Terminal Consciousness the AIDS virus will have no effect on you?

That's exactly what it means.

Does this mean that you can now forgo the precautions of safe sex if you're into spiritual things? I don't know. I believe that if you possessed sufficient spiritual clarity you could drink a quart of gasoline without ill effects. Are you going to attempt to drink gasoline any time soon?

I hope you said no.

The only way to know for sure that your consciousness can protect you from AIDS is to expose yourself to the virus and see what happens next.

Are you willing to do that?

I hope you said no.

As anyone can tell you who's been diagnosed as HIV-positive, the simple knowledge that you've been in contact with the virus can be a source of tremendous anxiety, anxiety that will certainly manifest itself negatively sooner or later. If not as AIDS, then as some other unwanted life experience.

It's certainly better to be without the virus than to be with it, at least as regards your peace of mind. Your consciousness will receive many challenges in the course of your life. There's no need to seek out distress and anxiety, as if you expected a shortage of such things.

And beyond all that is the fact that *there's no such thing as spiritual immunity to anything.* The finest spiritual thinkers I know have medical and accident insurance. Disease and injury are physical manifestations of conflicted beliefs. And if you've got any kind of consciousness worth having, it will constantly carry you forward into new and unexpected experiences that can produce mental conflict and confusion. Even *good* new experiences challenge your entrenched belief systems. So, you can always and at any time get yourself into a mental situation that can manifest as bodily discomfort and damage. There's no such thing as reaching a point in your spiritual evolution where body problems are impossible. You'd have to stop evolving entirely, to live without change, for that to happen; and spiritually aware people experience *more* change than do the unaware, not less.

So, wear an overcoat when it's cold out, don't get too much sun on your skin and don't share hypodermic needles with people. Take care of yourself. Never assume that your spiritual practices render you invulnerable. You might not like what happens.

Certainly there's no physical condition that can't be spiritually healed. You don't need to fear disease. But it's not a crisis of faith to suppose that your consciousness isn't quite evolved enough to enable you to give sight to the blind and walk on water. So, use your common sense.

Or to put it more clearly: *make sure your choice of action reflects what you really believe, not what you think you ought to believe.* Be smart now, show off later.

However, to be smart also means to be unafraid. If you commit yourself to safe sex practices, be sure you do it out of a sense of self-worth and as a gesture of love and regard to your sexual partner. And if you're acting out of fear, get rid of that belief system as soon as you can.

When you fear something, you choose it. The Law that turns thought into experience doesn't evaluate anything. Whatever you focus on, It produces. And fear is focus.

When we engage in a particular form of sex for the express purpose of avoiding something we fear, we're graphically and powerfully reinforcing whatever ideas are producing the fear. We can't escape responsibility for our thinking by carefully controlling our outer activity. That which we fear will come upon us, in one form or another, inevitably.

Come In: Do You Read Me?

Terminology can be misleading. If people make a bad choice of vocabulary in expressing an idea, it can create no end of communication problems. I've tried to make sure that the term *Terminal Consciousness* is interpreted positively and not to mean a death-wish or some kind of self-loathing.

A term that causes great distress when used in connection with the metaphysical causation of disease is the verb *to choose.*

It's become customary in the field of spiritual healing to say that someone chose to get sick and chose to die. People say, "I chose to have an auto accident" or "I chose to catch cold." I understand the purpose of such usage: the person wants to stay clear on the idea that he's responsible for his own experience. He wants, to use the common expression, to own his own shit.

But the above statements are simply inaccurate. I've seen people consciously choose to die, but absolutely nobody chooses to be sick. The idea that sick people have somehow decided to be sick gives rise to silly statements like, "Oh, you just want to be sick," or "You're not sick, you just think you are," remarks that make me want to lunge at the throat of whoever says them. Disease is the result of our choices, but not in such a silly, evil-fairy-godmother sort of way.

Belief: that's what we choose. We choose what we will believe. And since every belief manifests as an experience, we can create negative situations in our bodies by believing the wrong things. And we can dissolve those negative situations by embracing new beliefs.

Don't misunderstand: this is not to say that body problems come from believing bad things *about your body.* You don't have a bad back because you believed you were going to get one and you don't have acne because everybody told you that you would. *Any* false belief can manifest as an injury or bodily malfunction.

For instance: whenever I get overworked and my schedule becomes overburdened, I start to catch a cold. As soon as I notice that I'm sneezing more than is normal and sniffling a little, I realize that I've chosen to perceive my work agenda as disagreeable; I'm creating an excuse to stop. I immediately close my eyes and affirm: "I love my work. I'm grateful that so many people require my services. It is evidence of my success. I go forward to it joyfully," and other things to that effect. My symptoms vanish within the hour, and sometimes in mid-affirmation.

Notice that my affirmation in no way addressed my cold or its symptoms. The Infinite doesn't exactly know what a cold is. It only knows what I believe. *And It interprets every belief as a request.*

However, I have seen people choose to die. In fact, several of the people I've known who've died—from AIDS or from something else—were students of mine who had to face the fact that they were accepting death, because they knew as a result of their previous spiritual study that they could choose to stay if they wished.

You may say that it's a bad decision to choose to die. But if you think that, then you have a false perception of death. We fear death for ourselves and, well, we *disapprove* of death in other people. We see death as termination rather than as transition, as failure rather than as progress. As a child, the good sisters taught me that to die meant that one had gone to a glorious city in the sky to live with God and His saints and angels: it made me wonder why everybody acted like catastrophe had struck when someone died. Hey, he's in heaven, right? Saints and angels and eternal rewards? It sure sounded better than what I had to go through on a daily basis. What was all the boo-hooing about, I wondered?

Certainly we're sad when someone we love passes on, because we'll miss them and the good feelings they shared with us. We mourn for what we've lost. But it's spiritually incorrect to think that our friend has ceased to exist, and therefore incorrect to behave as if he had.

There are many theories about what happens to us after we die. It's a lot of fun to speculate about. And I have pet theories of my own. But it's not the purpose of this book to impose particular religious viewpoints. See death any way you choose. But I hope you see it as a moment of change, not as termination.

Here's what I think: I think dying is good for your health.

Eventually, for whatever reasons of our own, consciously or unconsciously, we decide to get out of here. It's a good thing. It would be terrible if we had to stay here forever with nothing to do. It's good to know that we can lay aside this body, this personality, this past history, when we decide we've gone as far as we can. There are different reasons to choose to go, some happy, some sad. People leave this world out of despair or out of joy, in defeat or in triumph. But the final result is always good: we're set free.

People die. We go through life pretending that this isn't so, and we're thunderstruck when someone we know announces that he's terminally ill. And we relate to dying people the same way we relate to winos begging on the street: as poor unfortunates going through a life experience that will never happen to us. *Thank God I'll never have to go through that,* we say about street beggars and about the terminally ill. We are going to live forever, we tell ourselves, unlike our unfortunate friend who has really, totally screwed up.

This pious condescension towards the dying is born of spiritual ignorance. In fact, we're usually at our most ignorant when faced with death because we so resolutely refuse to think about it at any other time.

Once you realize that every individual is in charge of his own death, you then begin to perceive a pattern in each death that you witness. In my healing groups, people were committed to becoming well. Most succeeded. But a few chose to go the other way. They chose to die. How do I know they made the choice? At first, I didn't. But after a few group members had died, I realized that each of them had put together an identical sequence of elements to support his passing.*

Specifically:

1 • Withdrawal from healing activities.

If the soon-to-be departed individual wants to pass on, he must withdraw from any kind of environment that supports a healing consciousness. If he's a participant in a spiritual healing group he must stop attending. Frequently he'll come up with very bizarre explanations of why he can't attend. If he has a friend of a metaphysical turn of mind who constantly encourages him to be well, he must get away from that friend.

2 • The Nurse Figure

Someone must come onto the scene to act as nurse and to run errands, keep house and generally take up the slack as the ill person goes into a decline. Sometimes the nurse is actually a health care professional, but more often it's just someone from the person's past. The nurse figure usually isn't someone who's been around very much. It's generally someone who appears out of the blue and with weird suddenness.

3 • Money Supply

The ailing person must acquire a source of cash that doesn't require them to work. Since they're withdrawing from life they can't simultaneously involve themselves with life by going to work every day. So, some alternative source of income must be established. (I've seen several people with AIDS end up getting a higher regular income from their disability payments than they were making at the jobs they quit.)

---

* Some people just told me they'd decided to die, just like that. Their symptoms returned soon after.

The curious aspect of all this is that these elements come into place *before* the person gets sick. It got to the point that I always knew when one of my students was going to pass away, because these things listed above would begin to appear in his life. Suddenly the student would stop attending the healing group for some very strange reason. ("I have to see clients on that night." "I can't find the new meeting place because it's dark out." "My lover needs the car that night.") After years of living alone, he'd abruptly move in with an old college chum. ("Sandra and I thought it would be fun to live together for a while.") And there would be a startling change in his source of income. ("I'm letting them give me early retirement because of my HIV status. The joke's on them, eh?") Whenever these items fell into place, I knew what was happening, even if the individual in question was healthy as a horse. The disease symptoms would appear soon after.

Be on the lookout for these warning signs. They will alert you to the real intentions of your friend. And as we'll see below, it's important that you support his choices, not the choices you think he ought to have made. And to do that, you must admit to yourself what's going on.

And there is a fourth element, one that arises after the disease symptoms have appeared:

4 • The patient returns home to visit his parents.
In every case I've witnessed, the impulse to return to the family is the prelude to the final passing. I won't analyze what this symbolizes. But it usually indicates that the patient is preparing to leave this world very soon.

None of this is to say that the patient knowingly plans his own demise and then sets up this scenario to support it. All this is usually instinctual. Quite often the patient doesn't recognize the direction in which he's moving himself. But at some level of his consciousness he does understand.

I call this an *unconscious agenda:* a purpose which the patient acts upon without acknowledging his purpose. It's very common for a person in Terminal Consciousness to act out an unconscious agenda. In fact, this same agenda described above appears over and over: withdrawal from healing activities, the acquisition of the Nurse Figure, the sudden, unprecedented supply of cash and, finally, the desire to stay at the parent's home.

I realize that all this will sound very cold and clinical to some people, particularly people who refuse to believe that a dying person has any control over his own death. Certainly, many people are offended by the idea that a person afflicted with a terminal illness is in any way responsible for his own situation.

But people who pass away are not the only ones affected by death. Those who care for them are also affected and must remain here to deal with their feelings after the patient is gone. I've seen too many people destroyed emotionally because they chose to care for a sick friend without knowing how to do it.

The gay men of my generation didn't think we'd have to deal with dying friends at this time in our lives. We thought that would be a challenge we'd face in another twenty years. None of us can be expected to be proficient at dealing with this kind of experience. We do it wrong, and we get hurt. I hope these observations, based on years of working with PWAs, will serve to guide people who have friends who "choose" not to recover from AIDS.

The only sex that is safe is that which is engaged in for good reasons, with a loving consciousness and a clear belief in the rightness of it.

The only life that is worth living is that which is engaged in for good reasons, with a loving consciousness and a clear belief in the rightness of it.

The only reason that reality is out there at all is to let us see what's going on in our consciousness. If we wonder what our belief systems are, we need only look at our outer experience. It is a mirror that reflects our consciousness back at us.

AIDS has come with a message, and the message is this:

"It's time to stop thinking ill of yourself. It's time to take your right and timely place in this world. You have Life's permission to live, or to die. It's time for you to choose."

If your body is to heal, you must heal your thinking.

Some people would rather die than change their minds. Are you one of them?

Do Your **Mindwork**
Part 8: How to Deal Wisely with the Dying

Sometimes the events of life unfold in such a way that we end up nursing someone into their death; a friend or a relative is leaving this world and for one reason or another we're the most likely person to help him through it. To nurse a dying individual can be a fulfilling and enlightening experience, or it can be a personal catastrophe, depending on how you handle it.

Here's a checklist of things that will make the experience a healthy one for you.

1 • Don't identify with the dying.

You're not dying, he is. He's leaving, you're staying: that's the deal. And even if you think you might die of the same cause some day, you're not dying today, he is. Remember whose experience is whose.

Relate to him as another person not as some extension of yourself.

2 • Decide what you're going to get out of it.

Selflessness is a suspicious virtue. Quite often it's really self-destructiveness wearing a halo. If you decide to nurse a dying person, make sure you're clear as to your own motives. Too often when we're faced with a dying friend, we "drop everything" and commit 100% of our time to his care, even if he doesn't need us around all the time. You might reasonably do this if the person is particularly dear to you and you want to make sure you get as much time as you can with him before he departs. But too often we nurse our sick friends and relatives out of a morbid sense of obligation brought on by a morbid fear of death.

You have a life. It's good that you do. Remember to live it. Don't feel guilty that he's leaving and you're staying.

Health and death are not opposites; they are different expressions of the same process. There's a good reason for his passing and a good reason for your continuing presence on earth. Both creative impulses deserve to be honored, the one the takes him away and the one that keeps you here.

3 • Support his experience

Too many people involved in spiritual study think that the proper way to relate to a dying person is to "talk him out of it." We try to browbeat him into wellness. Every encounter becomes an opportunity to pontificate about Spirit and healing and the power of belief.

This is crass ignorance. We're telling our friend that he's doing something wrong, that he shouldn't die. And we're committing the gravest offense possible in this universe of Spirit: we are seeking to interpose ourselves between someone and his God.

Furthermore—and I speak from painful experience—the attempt to force such a change in the thinking of someone else can be emotionally devastating for us. We're wasting our time. His decision is made and our well-intentioned harangues about life and healing have no impact on his thought at all. We're setting ourselves up for a crushing letdown.

It was never your job to run his life for him and it still isn't. Don't try to change his mind. It's none of your business. And nothing bad is happening to him. He's just dying. Acknowledge it.

Support him in *his* choices, not in the choices you think he ought to have made.

4 • Don't become a prop in his pageant

Dying people seem to fall into one of two camps.

For some people, dying is an enlightening experience. They're pleased to be going, even excited, and in their last days they rise to a level of nobility and emotional honesty that's a blessing to everyone around them.

Others use their death as a weapon.

Their terminal condition lends them a morally superior status which they use to manipulate everyone around them. They use the fact of their impending death as a way of sticking it to everyone against whom they bear a grudge, especially parents and siblings. Their dying turns into a five-act opera and they get everybody in the house jumping through hoops.

Watch out for the latter. They can take you down with them. Deal with your dying friend with the same integrity with which you deal with anyone else. Say what you need to say to them. Say *everything* you need to say to them; this isn't the time to leave any business unfinished, or to be tactfully silent.

Certainly you'll give anyone some slack when they're in a bad situation. If a friend is in bad financial straits or getting a divorce, you'll allow him some bad behavior. If he's sick and dying, you'll allow him that much more. But at no time should you allow anyone to abuse you, manipulate you or to interfere with the healthy maintenance of your life. If your dying friend tries any tricks with your head, tell him to cut the crap. You'll be glad you did, and he might be glad, too.

Too often, caregivers are relieved to see their patient die. For months they look haggard and downtrodden, and then at the funeral, they're radiant. "He's *finally* dead!" they seem to say. These people didn't set the proper boundaries with their dying loved ones. They didn't say, "Oh, cut the crap." They allowed themselves to be jerked around.

This isn't the way we want it to be. We don't want to be sad while we take care of our friend and jubilant when he's dead. We want to enjoy him while he's here and be sad when he's gone.

To do this, we must hold him to a high standard of behavior, the same to which we hold ourselves. Don't take a superior attitude towards the dying, but don't let them take a superior attitude towards you. 100% of Spirit is within each one of you, expressing Itself in different ways.

5 • Don't Make Funerals Your Hobby

The AIDS epidemic has added a bizarre new twist to the kind of "fake friendship" described in Chapter Four: fake friendship with the dead. Gay men will claim to have "dearly loved" deceased people who, in truth, they never had anything to do with in life. Some gay men have taken up the practice of attending as many memorial services as they can, tearfully mourning the passing of "dear friends" who, needless to say, are in no position to challenge that description of themselves.

Gay men have also come to indulge in a kind of morbid one-upsmanship as regards *how many* dead friends they have. "I have five friends who've died of AIDS," says one. "Oh, I have twelve," says another in response. The numbers can get pretty outlandish, especially if cocktails are being served. I remember a conversation in which someone claimed to have *thirty-seven* dear friends who had died of AIDS. Looking then at the angry, depressed, sarcastic little man who'd made that extravagant claim, the thought occurred to me—sadly, and a bit uncharitably—that he'd probably never had thirty-seven friends of any kind, let alone such a surplus of friends that he could lose thirty-seven of them to the disease.

The world is full of living people who will welcome your love and who will love you just as you are. There's no need to construct an imaginary social life peopled by deceased individuals who can never disappoint you, never hurt you and never refute your claims of deep affection.

to
Set Another Free

AFFIRMATION

There is nowhere to be but within Spirit.

Everything is One Thing. Every place is the One Place. Each individual soul is the expression of the One Soul.

I am right now a part of everything. And everything is where I am. There is no separation. There is no point at which I leave off and the rest of Life begins. Everything is One Thing.

Therefore, my friend and I can't be separated from each other, because we both must eternally be within Spirit. There is nowhere for him to go that isn't within Spirit.

I can release him into the hands of that Presence, knowing that It will take care of him as it now takes care of me. My friend can't go anywhere that Spirit isn't. And the Divine Presence that fills his life right now is the same Presence that will always be there for him. His relationship with this Presence can never change.

His time here is done. Mine is not. But he and I are complete. All business is settled, all accounts are paid. And we are both free to move on in our separate directions, within the One Life that is the only Life either of us will ever know or need.

Chapter Eight

Send That Bitch Away
How to Be Healed of AIDS

Sweetness and light never healed anything.
—*Raymond Charles Barker*

When the first version of this book appeared on the stands, there was very little popular literature on spiritual healing and virtually none on the healing of AIDS. The greatest teachers of spiritual healing in the 20th century—Ernest Holmes, Emmet Fox, Thomas Troward and others—were known only to participants in Religious Science, Science of Mind or other New Thought ministries and their written works appeared in hard-to-find and not-very-attractively-bound editions from publishers who regarded them as low-end products.

Now, six years later, book stores have whole sections on spiritual healing and as much as a full shelf devoted specifically to AIDS. The person with AIDS who seeks information about spiritual healing would have been alone in a wilderness six years ago, but today has the opposite problem: he's inundated with information from dozens of spiritual writers and teachers, who frequently contradict each other on crucial points. The question now isn't "Does anyone out there know anything about spiritual healing?" Today the question is "Who of all these people knows what he's talking about and who's full of shit?" Needless to say, a person diagnosed with AIDS feels pressed for time. He

121

doesn't have a few years to waste following the recommendations of a well-intentioned goofball, or of a greedy charlatan. He wants the right stuff right away.

Every spiritual teaching on the market has come up with a system for healing AIDS, or at least for dealing with the consequences of the disease. These programs have come into existence for the same two motives, mixed together in different proportions in the different teachings:

1 • a sincere desire to help, and

2 • a crafty understanding of what the public is buying.

This combination of caring and opportunism has its good side and its bad side: it has served to promote non-medical healing concepts to the general public and to create standing organizations to continue that work; it has also produced a lot of sloppy thinking, vague theorizing and the promotion of healing gimmickry based more on sales potential than on any actual results produced.

A good question to ask any teacher of healing is, "What do you mean by *healing?*" If you find it hard to get a straight answer out of him (or her), or if the "healing" in question turns out to be a nicey-nicey, psychological, emotional kind of healing—instead of the material healing of the body—you might try a different teacher. A "spiritual healer" whose clients die with the same regularity as people who don't resort to spiritual healing really ought to get himself into a line of work where he can be useful; waiting tables, perhaps, or managing apartment buildings.

Let me be very clear about what I mean by "healing." I'm talking about *the material healing of the physical body in response to the right use of consciousness.*

Is such a thing possible? Of course it is. It happens every day. People have been doing it for as long as there have been people.

What kind of healings have I witnessed? A lot. I've seen the lesions of Kaposi's Sarcoma disappear from people's legs and never return. I've seen walking skeletons return to normal body weight and daily routine. I've seen people come out of comas and return to health. You'll hear more about some of these people as you read on.

Does that sort of thing seem impossible? It's not even unusual. It's normal. Anybody can do it.

Let me also make clear that in my discussion of the healing of AIDS, as in all areas of my teaching, I never stray from my field of expertise. So-called spiritual teachers blithely discuss the immune system and other medical concepts from their podiums, even though they have no real expertise in medical science beyond that of any informed layman. Likewise, they refer to "neuroses" and "codependency" and "addiction" and "trauma" as if they possessed degrees in psychology.

My expertise is in how the Infinite operates through the individual. That's what I know about. So, you won't find in this book any technical descriptions of your immune system and how it works, because I don't know any more about that than you do. Probably less.

Furthermore, all of the information below on healing is taken from direct personal experience. None of it represents pet theories of mine that I think you should go try out. You'll read only about what real people with AIDS did in order to be healed. You'll read only about what they made work.

Be clear also that if you're a person with AIDS who wants to attempt spiritual healing, you're not really pressed for time. If you sincerely decide to remain in this life and go forward into the future here instead of somewhere else, then that decision will dominate your experience because it will instantaneously become the decision that the Infinite honors and supports.

Ah, which brings us to the possibly unwelcome subject of the Infinite.

Which is to say: God.

You Can't Heal Your Life

A remark that's been made more than once regarding the first version of this book is, "I liked everything you said until you got into all that spiritual stuff in Part Three." The obvious response is that the agreeable stuff in Parts One and Two can't possibly make any sense *without* the "spiritual stuff" in Part Three.

Many gay men absolutely detest any discussion of life's spiritual dimension. Their distaste for the subject, they say, derives from the fact that gay people have been treated so horribly by organized religion. This is one of those oh-so-politically-correct explanations that we should learn to suspect when we hear it come out of our mouths. I believe that the gay man's distaste for spiritual ideas comes from a different source.

Can we put this tactfully?

No? We can't?

Okay, then: *gay men are control freaks.*

Okay, so not all gay men are control freaks, and if you're one of the exceptions, hooray for you. But it is a problem for us. It comes from the way we grow up.

A closeted teenager usually becomes a little too clever for his own good. Cleverness is his principal survival tactic. "Can't catch *me!*" he says with a mischievous grin. Cleverness is a trait we admire in teenagers, but clever adults can be rather tiresome. I believe that the cleverness that protects the closeted gay youth from detection is a painful liability in the adult gay man. I believe this need to be clever is why so many gay men become experts in culture and style, why they are fascinated by show business and why so much gay conversation takes the form of sarcastic repartee.

Lots of gay men are extremely well-read and intellectual for the same reason. They hold the world at bay by being the smartest guys in the room. Intelligence is native to all humans, but intellectualism is a kind of highbrow cleverness that very articulately compares This Thing to That Thing in a way that truly benefits no one except maybe some publisher somewhere and perhaps supplies a few laughs at cocktail parties.

Clever teenagers tend to grow up to be very hardworking, very entertaining, very lonely and very nervous. They need to micro-manage everything in their lives because they've blundered into adulthood without any sense that anything could simply work out for them without any manipulation on their part. They distrust their world.

I believe that many gay men dislike discussing spiritual matters because it alarms them to think that there are important aspects of their lives that they can't get their hands on and control.

Furthermore, they dislike the fact that spirituality requires them to give up part of their rational faculties and surrender to a spiritual Power which they can only partially comprehend. Certainly spiritual study requires us also to think logically and scientifically about spiritual questions. We must refuse to believe in something without real evidence to support the belief. *But to create that evidence we must have faith in Something Unseen.*

Sooner or later, the spiritual seeker must perform an experiment in which he chooses to believe in something just so he can see what happens as a result. This is what's known as a leap of faith. It's not a control freak's idea of a good time. Control freaks aren't into leaping anywhere for any reason. They're afraid of being wrong. They're afraid someone will be watching. They're afraid of being embarrassed.

People who are chronically afraid of being embarrassed end up in Terminal Consciousness pretty early on. What is the future, after all, if not an endless series of opportunities to make a fool of yourself?

Control freaks are also put off by the silliness of many people who dabble in mysticism. A lot of spiritual seekers make their leap of faith way too soon—like after *one* seminar—and this leads them into all kinds of eccentricities. The control freak latches on to the goofy behavior of spiritual dilettantes to justify his own refusal to investigate the subject in depth.

But when a person contracts AIDS, these anally retentive defense mechanisms must be set aside. The cost of giving them up is nowhere near as great as the cost of keeping them in place. If you want your healing, there is a price to pay. The message from the Infinite is clear and simple:

Get over yourself, little one.

But, in deference to this distaste for things spiritual, I'll continue to avoid the use of the word "God." I'll call It something else like "Spirit," which is a nice, vague term with a touch of the mystical about it (unlike the term "Infinite," which makes this sound like an astronomy textbook). You can conceive of Spirit any way you choose. Though, I'll warn you, if you conceive of Spirit as a giant human being of either gender, you'll create problems for yourself.

Let's establish the basic characteristics of this Infinite Spirit:

1 • It can do anything, provided that the proposed action doesn't violate Its own nature. As Dr. Barker once put it, "God can't commit suicide." Which is to say, Spirit can't stop being Spirit. All demands made upon It will be answered in accord with It's own nature.

2 • It can't say, "no." It can only say, "yes." So, It can't withhold anything from you.

3 • It has no opinion of you. Or to put it another way, since you're part of It, It has to like you.

4 • It turns your beliefs into experience whether you want It to or not.

5 • It knows everything.

6 • It is everything.

It's within neither the scope nor the tone of this little book to examine in detail why any of this is so. If the subject interests you, check out the suggested reading list in the back. It will direct you to books that explore this area of inquiry more fully. For now, just try to get your mind around the idea that this Presence has whatever it takes to heal you and is incapable of denying you your healing.

And now, here's something you need to know about you:

You don't have the power to heal yourself.

Human beings don't have the power to heal themselves. They don't have the power to heal each other, either.

Spirit heals. And only Spirit heals.

A gay man who's used to confronting the world with his cleverness instead of with his heart and mind will just hate this kind of statement. In fact, the general perception of spiritual healing among the gay men I've spoken to about it is that it's some kind of biofeedback-like process wherein by meditating, affirming and visualizing, the patient sends brain waves or something down into his body that force the cell tissues and blood chemistry to behave differently.

Booga-booga.

This science fiction explanation for spiritual healing is why medical doctors are so offended by the whole thing. This explanation is an attempt by too-terribly-clever gay men to use spiritual healing without using Spirit. They want to keep the process within the bounds of what they already believe to be true. They want to have their healing without having to expand their thinking.

No wonder so much quackery and cheap theatrics surround the simple business of spiritual healing, if the clients—and quite often their teachers—don't understand this essential and fundamental concept: *You can't heal yourself.*

Now, you may want to stop right here. Many people would rather die than think this way, and many do just that. You may want to go on thinking of spiritual healing as something that isn't really a matter of Spirit at all; it's something in the body chemistry, it's the manipulation of emotions, it's waves in your cerebrum. You may be a little put off by the idea of praying to—let's call It what It is this once—God.

My response would be that if you think praying to God is silly, I think *praying to your brain* is really ridiculous.

The biofeedback-in-the-brain conception of spiritual healing shows itself clearly in the people who've embraced it. They're the ones who try to use spiritual techniques as a kind of magical version of medical treatment; they try to use meditation and affirmation to control their symptoms, to produce improved test results, to raise their energy level or their t-cell count, as if prayers and spiritual mind treatments were the mental equivalents of pills and injections. Certainly human beings can produce some such effects through use of will power. But no one will experience a complete spiritual healing who uses only the power of his individual mind, and that merely to mitigate evils. Spiritual healing works for those who abandon such control tactics, admit their helplessness, and surrender themselves to Spirit for healing. (Surrendering yourself to Spirit doesn't mean being passive.)

I've seen many people heal from AIDS. Many of them did me the honor of being my clients. And in the case of each one of my clients, the first thing I had to do was wrestle him to the floor (so to speak) and force him to give up the idea that he was somehow going to heal *himself.* To try and heal yourself is a burdensome and counterproductive approach to healing since it places impossible demands upon the patient.

We don't heal ourselves. We allow ourselves to be healed by a Infinite Power. Big difference.

The person who approaches spiritual healing as a do-it-yourself, tinkering kind of thing very soon stumbles out of spiritual study and into pop psychology. All of a sudden he wants to forgive his parents and be more loving and avoid criticizing others, etc., etc., etc., with the idea in mind that these psychological improvements will cause his body to heal. By all reports, this approach has not had a particularly good success rate for People with AIDS. It's a good thing to forgive your parents and to be more loving and not to criticize and all that; everybody ought to strive to do these things all the time anyway, right? But crying at weekend seminars and oozing with expressions of unconditional love will probably do very little to heal your body because your disease probably isn't caused by problems in those areas. To try and heal a terminal illness by making adjustments to your personality is like a pilot trying to avert a plane crash by cleaning the windshield. There's a more general, systemic problem that won't be helped by changing the view.

The painful difficulty brought out by the change-your-personality-and-you'll-heal school of spiritual healing is this: what if the healing doesn't happen? It could only mean that the *patient* has failed, that he was unable to become *good enough* to be healed. He is, by implication, a bad person, or at least not a very successful one. Or, the other explanation would be that the mind and body aren't directly connected; It's been said to me about recently-deceased people who'd attempted spiritual healing, "He healed his consciousness, but he couldn't heal his body." That's impossible. The body is a physical representation of the consciousness. If the consciousness is healed, the body *must* follow suit.

It's more likely that people who fail in their spiritual healings do so because they heal many psychological and emotional problems without dealing with *the larger problem of belief.* They cleaned the windshield instead of repairing the engine. Specifically, they didn't change their attitude towards their own future.

In fact, meddling with your personality in such a period of crisis is the worst kind of self-defeating behavior, since the impulse to personally manage every element of your healing is exactly the opposite of the needed state of receptivity that healing demands.

Spiritual healing is not psychotherapy. If it was, terminally ill people could be healed by going to their shrinks once a week. Spiritual healing makes use of a Power that transcends your individual mind, personality and capacities. If you insist on trying to heal yourself through some vaguely-conceived biological process triggered by your brain, you're setting yourself up for a miserable time and probable failure. Rather than identifying your bad personality as the cause of your disease, realize that your personality problems *and* your disease both proceed from the same false belief systems. They are both manifestations. The one doesn't cause the other.

Can psychotherapy be helpful to someone who's pursuing a spiritual healing? You bet it can. It can help a lot. But then, so can medicine, and a good night's sleep and intelligent exercise.

This is not to suggest that as you seek your healing you ought to be passive and uninvolved. Surrendering to Spirit doesn't mean inaction. You're going to have to be creative, flexible, patient and very, very, very insistent. But don't confuse your own self-care activities with the healing Power of Spirit. When you engage in a spiritual healing, you're turning yourself over to a Power that is infinitely greater than anything you could produce on your own. And any health-related activities in which you choose to engage are only a tiny part of a larger coordinated movement of healing that is being performed by a Power which is not limited to the confines of your body.

This is all sounding a little spooky, isn't it?

Well, it's not spooky. It's fun.

But it's not "pop biology."

Fingering the Culprit

In many people's minds, the biggest obstacle to spiritual healing may be it's basic premise: namely, that the patient is personally responsible for his own disease. This just isn't a nice thing to say about a sick person. The idea that your beliefs become your reality is all well and good if we're talking about money or employment or relationships. But when we get into the area of disease and death it seems like kind of a mean idea. It's much kinder to perceive our sick friend as a victim of external factors.

But the victim perception can't heal anything. Until the patient is ready to accept the idea that something in his thinking is cause to the disease, then he'll never be ready to accept responsibility for his own healing. And besides: he *is* responsible. 100% responsible. If that offends you, get over it. He's responsible.

Relax, it's not as bad as it sounds. However, this concept is often misinterpreted in distressing ways: the patient hates himself, he wants to die, he deserves what he's getting, his mind contains something really nasty and ugly that is manifesting as a disease and, most ridiculous of all, he's only imagining that he's sick.

But the belief systems that manifest as diseases don't have to be evil. Just because the situations they produce are negative doesn't mean that the beliefs themselves are negative. To produce a bad situation in your life, a belief only needs to be *false*. The moral evaluation of good or bad is irrelevant. Negative life situations aren't all caused by *negative* belief systems, but they are all caused by lies.

A mother who's fretting over her sick child will tell herself all kinds of lies. "Oh, the poor, sick little thing. He's helpless against this disease. I guess it's the will of God," and like that. Certainly no one could call this "negative thinking." It's entirely good, decent, loving thinking. But it's all lies. He's not a poor, sick little thing, he's a perfect expression of Spirit. And he's not helpless against the disease; he can choose to be healed any time he wants to. And it's not the will of God; it's the false belief of humans.

This is why some spiritual practitioners get reputations for being aloof, emotionally cool people. Because they don't sympathize. It's their job to see the Truth behind the condition, not to commiserate compassionately at the level of the problem. Commiseration is well-intended and kind, but it heals nothing.

There's a difference between sympathy and understanding. Understanding supports the healing, sympathy supports the problem.

The first question asked by the PWA seeking spiritual healing always seems to be, "Why do I have AIDS?" The idea apparently is that, since disease proceeds from false belief, the cure must be to figure out what that false belief is. This is another attempt to turn spiritual healing into psychotherapy. In psychotherapy, the challenge in healing an emotional problem is to get to the bottom of it, to bring the cause of the problem up into the light of day. However effective this might be in the practice of psychology, it has nothing to do with spiritual healing. Many of the people I've seen heal from AIDS had no idea why they got it in the first place. (They knew *how* they got it, of course.) Some of them didn't figure it out until after their healing was well-established. And many of them who were sure from the start what belief structure was producing their disease found out later that they were completely wrong.

There's no need to know what mental situation is cause to your disease. It doesn't matter. This isn't like medical practice wherein the cause must be pinpointed before treatment can begin.

You're turning your problem over to Spirit so that Spirit can heal you. And It already knows where the problem is and what to do about it. So you don't need to. The idea that you must dig around in your mind until you find the offending belief system brings us right back to that dreary idea that *you* are making the healing happen.

The "Why Do I Have AIDS?" question is also a brilliant delaying tactic. The person who seeks a spiritual healing knows somewhere in his heart of hearts that he's going to have to make some changes in the way he thinks and relates to life. The average too-terribly-clever gay man isn't comfortable with that prospect, so he turns his healing quest into a too-terribly-clever process of figuring out the mental causation of his illness. It's an engrossing waste of time.

"How can I be healed?" is a more interesting question,

and a much more important one. In the area of spiritual healing, finding the cause of the problem doesn't heal anything; but finding the solution does.

How do you find the solution without first finding the cause? Simple: The solution is the opposite of the problem.

Read that again: *The solution is the opposite of the problem.*

The Numbers Game

The British statesman Benjamin Disraeli said there are only three kinds of falsehood: "Lies, damned lies, and statistics."

People who are uncertain about their future tend to obsess over statistics. They want to know the rate of violent crime in their neighborhood, the incidence of certain diseases in people of their age and culture, their family's medical histories, the number of people who find a spouse after the age of forty, the average period of time it takes an unemployed person to find a job, the official poverty level, the odds of winning the lottery, the number of rat hairs permitted in hot dogs, and so on and so forth.

Certainly the AIDS crisis has generated an ongoing hurricane of statistics, and many gay men have become morbidly obsessed with numbers and data.

Years ago a newspaper headline announced that 98% of the people with AIDS would die of it. How they reached that figure I don't know. My heart sank when I saw this on the newsstand because it was a Wednesday and I knew that our healing group that night would revolve entirely around the fear that this headline would provoke in some of the participants.

Sure enough, the subject was raised immediately. One of the members complained that the kind of statistics presented by the newspaper headline always upset him horribly and undermined the healing consciousness he tried so hard to develop in himself. Several others agreed vociferously. 98%! Imagine that!

I was preparing to launch into a long, boring harangue

about the healing power of Spirit and the individual's experience of his own consciousness when one of the group
members, bless his dark little heart, raised an eyebrow and
said, "Well, you guys are in the 2% that live, so what are you
worried about?"

There was a confused silence.

They hadn't thought of that.

Neither had I.

This is how people inevitably respond to statistics.
They assume that they're in the bad part. If 98% of the people
with AIDS are going to die of it, then you assume you're in
the 98%. We never ask, "Who are the 2% who live? How
come they don't die? How do you get to be one of them?"
We're geared towards the assumption of the negative. If
we're told we've got a fifty-fifty chance, we place ourselves
in the doomed fifty.

Nowhere is this tendency more in evidence than in the
lives of HIV-positive people who are asymptomatic, that is,
people who have no disease symptoms, but whose blood
tests indicate that they've been exposed to the virus.

To be HIV-positive is a bizarre kind of situation in that
you can be diagnosed as sick when there's nothing wrong
with you. In HIV-positive cases, doctors often prescribe
powerful medication with corrosive side effects even though
the patient is suffering no symptoms of anything at all. The
medical treatment often is based on an assumption of what
will happen to the patient, an assumption born of statistical
evidence of what happened to other people who were HIV-
positive.

The principle symptom of HIV-positivity is *worry*.
People with the HIV diagnosis spend most of their spare
mental time entertaining dire possibilities about their future.

A great deal of energy is expended in worrying about
whether or not to get tested in the first place. I've had many
clients in my practice who are overwhelmed with terror
about the findings of their HIV tests and yet have no idea
why they got tested in the first place, except to say that they

were surrounded by people who encouraged them to get tested, as if getting tested was somehow civic-minded or patriotic. Now they're trapped in a mental spiral of fear based on health statistics taken from the life experiences of others with that same condition.

(One individual of my acquaintance who'd tested positive said to me, "If I'm going to get AIDS in three years, I'd have been better off just waking up sick one morning. Now, I'll wake up sick one morning after three years of worrying." Of course, I slapped his wrist for assuming that disease was inevitable, but his point was interesting.)

Doctors encourage people to get tested. It's entirely appropriate that they do; the doctors want to begin treatment of the patient as soon as possible to ensure, from the medical viewpoint, that the greatest chance for health and long life is afforded. They also want to assemble reliable statistics on the rate of infection and the projected financial impact it will have on the health care system.

But many, many HIV-positive people refuse to be treated medically for their condition. They may decide to make certain healthful changes in their habits—they stop drinking alcohol, stop smoking, reduce stress levels, learn to eat intelligently, get some exercise—but these are all things that everybody ought to be doing all the time anyway, right?

Do you want me to tell you whether or not to get tested? Well, I won't. It's not my job in life to make decisions for you. Probably you're surrounded by people—doctors, activists and friends—who think it *is* their job in life to make decisions for you, or at least to browbeat you into making the decisions they consider correct. That's okay. They're nice folks. They're concerned for your well-being. Find a polite way to say, "Thanks for your input. Now, shutup." Because ultimately it's you who must decide whether or not to be tested. And you must decide for your own individual reasons. Because ultimately it's you, not they, who must live with the emotional consequences of your test results.

If you're considering getting tested, I suggest you first

find an answer to this question: *What will you do with the information?* Suppose you test positive? What will you do with the information? Don't wait until after the results are in to ponder this question.

And in the end, don't do what's right. Do what's right for *you*.

As for all those statistics: it's the basic premise of the new spirituality that each person experiences his or own consciousness *and nothing else.* Statistics are a record of what other people have done with their consciousness. Statistics are the consequences of other people's belief systems. How much your statistics will resemble theirs will be determined by the extent to which you choose to think the way they did. And that's up to you. If you will learn to think differently, you'll have a different life experience that produces different statistics.

All this comes too little and too late for people who have already tested positive. You're already dealing with this, and your reaction is somewhere within the spectrum of sighing optimism to morbid panic. You don't need to answer the question *What will you do with the information?*

The question you must answer is: *Are you sick?*

Medically, to be antibody positive is to be sort-of-but-not-exactly-sick-but-anyway-you-will-be-someday-probably-so-it's-the-same-thing. It's a little bit speculative. Different research reports have issued different estimates as to what percentage of HIV-positive people will develop AIDS and what percentage will not. AIDS activists seeking to get our funding agencies to produce more money for research and education will say that *everybody* who's antibody positive will get AIDS.

So, you're in limbo. Limbo is not a pleasant place to be. But how you get out of it is really up to you. *Are you sick?* Don't ask your doctor. As long as that positive test result is in place, he can't ethically or in good conscience tell you you're fine.

But in spiritual healing, a doctor's opinion is not given

much weight. Perhaps this is another aspect of the process that physicians dislike. They are no longer the final authority. In fact, they're not any kind of authority. Someone who claims he's healing through Spirit but who keeps running back to his doctor for confirmation is kidding himself. Who's doing the healing? Where has he placed his faith? In God or the doctor?

Many teachers of spiritual healing who work with AIDS patients proudly proclaim that they have "medical evidence" that spiritual healing works. Aside from the fact that this is highly unlikely—the medical profession has rather severe guidelines as to what constitutes real evidence—it seems counterproductive and a sign of bad faith.

There's a creeping misperception within the spiritual healing movement that this kind of healing will really have proven its worth when medical doctors confirm its effectiveness. This is like thinking that rock music will have proven itself to be a true art form when Luciano Pavarotti sings "Purple Haze." Not to speak ill of Mr. Pavarotti, but does any rock singer feel incomplete without his blessing? I personally couldn't care less whether or not doctors ever give their blessing to spiritual healing. It has nothing to do with them. And to determine the effectiveness of spiritual healing through the standards of material medicine is pointless.

For instance, many seekers of spiritual healing announce that it is their goal to become HIV antibody negative. This is a strange ambition. Why on earth would you want to *remove* an antibody from your system? My friends who are health care providers tell me that antibodies are good things.

The intention to become antibody negative through spiritual healing is another attempt to operate by doctors' rules. Since the antibody positive diagnosis is considered a disease situation, then healing it must be a matter of producing the opposite test result.

I've heard tell of people who've become antibody negative through spiritual practices. But in all the healed people I've known, none have made this claim. The goal of spiritual healing is to produce a healthy, fully alive human being, not to produce a set of test results to impress a doctor.

Instead of claiming there is "medical evidence" that spiritual healing works, perhaps we ought to simply accept the *physical* evidence. When a person of deteriorated physical condition does a mental about-face and becomes a smiling, energetic, healthy individual, that's enough evidence for me. What a medical researcher might say about him after running some cells under a microscope is of no interest to me at all.

And besides, I've seen laboratory results conflict outrageously with the reality of a patient's condition. One of our group members appeared one night and announced, greatly amused, that his new test results indicated that he had *no* t-cells. Zero. Zilch. *Nada*. He was amused because he felt healthier and more vibrant than he ever had in his life.

"But how does it feel to be told this?" I asked him.

"Oh, honey," he said, "it's where I've always wanted to be. Out on that runway, all by myself!"

Periodically in my healing groups, someone—usually a new member—would say something like, "I'm having my blood tests run tomorrow, and I know the news will be good."

The other members—some of whom had made the same pronouncement and lived to regret it—would all turn to me in unison.

I'd say: "If you *know* the news will be good, why are you having the tests done at all?"

"I want my doctor to see what I'm accomplishing here."

"Ah, uh-huh. You want to share this with your doctor, do you?"

A week would pass and, sure enough, the test results were not good at all. His GQ-cells were down or his queerocytes or whatever, and he'd be in a panic.

A person with a medically incurable disease who desires a spiritual healing must eventually lose interest in his medical data entirely. Don't think you can rejoice in the hopeful data and ignore the scary data. If you give weight to the one, you will automatically give weight to the other.

Here's a story about someone who learned how to deal with input from his medical advisor:

Sorta True Story #7

Jethro's Blood

An AIDS patient's doctor will test his blood regularly to monitor the production of certain immune-related cells. Many people with AIDS become "data junkies," determining their expectations for happiness and long life by the numbers produced by these tests.

My friend—we'll call him Jethro (he actually has one of those country-type names)—realized one day that his emotional states had come entirely under the domination of his test results: if the numbers went up he was elated and looked forward to a long life. If they went down he was panic-stricken by the approach of death.

His physical health, he finally realized, was always the same despite the direction taken by the latest batch of tests.

Jeth was a spiritual student and, although he accepted medical treatment for his condition, he knew that his healing came from Spirit, not from chemical medicines. He also knew that this morbid dependence on numbers and tests, and the resulting mood swings it produced, would prove disastrous for his health if he continued to indulge it.

At his next monthly checkup the doctor, who is a very fine person, began to rattle off Jethro's latest results. Numbers, numbers, numbers. This is up, this is down.

"Okay, *hold* it!" said Jeth. "Just stop."

The doctor blinked in astonishment.

"Is there anything in those tests that I should be alarmed about?" said Jeth. "Or even concerned about?"

The doctor looked down at his papers. He thought for a second. "Well, no," he said. "I suppose there isn't."

"So, you'd say my test results are—what? Fine? Good?"

The doctor thought again. "I would say that your blood counts look just fine."

"Okay, then," Jeth said, "from now on, that's all I want to hear from you. Good, fine, whatever. I don't want numbers, I want *your medical opinion*. If you ever find anything in there that indicates that we need to change my medication or my diet or my work schedule, then you tell me and we'll talk about it. But you're ruining my life with these numbers."

You might expect the doctor to defend his turf and insist that things go on as before. But actually he liked the idea.

Jeth is still alive and very healthy. And he continues to allow his doctors to collect the medical data that they need. But when Jeth is at his AIDS support group, when anyone begins to express fear about lowering blood counts, Jeth says proudly, "I have no idea what my blood counts are."

This astonishes people. "Don't you have them checked?"

"Of course. But I don't ask about the results. I feel fine, so they must be okay."

This is usually greeted with silence.

"So, how are you?" he'll then say to someone.

"Well, my t-cells went down fifty points."

"Yeah, well, how *are* you?"

"I guess I'm sick," they will say.

"Do you feel sick?"

"No, I feel fine."

"Well, then," Jeth will say, "maybe you ought to *say* you're fine."

Among his fellow AIDS patients, Jeth has a reputation for being eccentric. However, he also has a reputation for having wonderful, warm working relationships with doctors that everybody else complains are bastards. He also has a reputation for not dying.

One night, Jeth's lover had a crisis of faith. He wondered if Jeth's passage through AIDS could end happily.

"Do you ever wonder if this is all nonsense?" he asked Jeth. "What if it's just media hokum? What if no one has ever been spiritually healed of AIDS?"

Jeth shrugged. "Well then, I guess I'll have to be the first," he said.

*To preserve one's health by too strict
a regimen is in itself a tedious malady.*
— *La Rochefoucauld*

The future is yours, if you'll have it. You don't have to go out and make your future; it's already yours. You don't have to stay here, of course. You can go pursue your future in whatever kind of life comes after this one. What will that life be like? I wouldn't know. But we'll all find out eventually.

If you want to stay here, you must give yourself a reason. Being afraid of death isn't a reason to live. Things that make you feel happy and worthy are reasons to live.

In spiritual healing, the opposite of the problem is the solution. Spiritual healing doesn't deal with the details of the problem. That's what physicians and psychologists do. Spiritual healing deals only with the desired good. A spiritual practitioner heals a problem by affirming the opposite of the problem, not by trying to manipulate the facts of the case. The answer to poverty is abundance, the answer to loneliness is Oneness, the answer to frustration is self-expression, the answer to disease is wholeness, the answer to impending death is …the future.

It's difficult for me to decide how far to go in explaining spiritual healing. I know my audience. I know there are many gay men out there who desire a healing but who froth at the mouth when spirituality is discussed. I don't want to lose you. I respect your skepticism. I even respect your cynicism.

But the first step in spiritually healing a medically incurable disease is to admit that you don't have a solution to your problem. If you had a solution, you wouldn't be reading this chapter, would you? The solution will have to come from somewhere outside the boundary of your assumptions. To find that solution, you'll have to step outside the boundary of your assumptions and have a look.

This isn't a matter of becoming wildly eccentric. Many would-be spiritual seekers think they're stepping outside the boundary of their assumptions when all they're really doing is acting goofy. They embark on a search for their healing and next thing you know, they're trying to trance channel Gloria Swanson to help them communicate with UFO aliens who have a cure for AIDS. I wish them luck. I really do.

But you're more the Joe Friday type. You just want the facts, ma'am.

Well, here they are:

1 • Get Clear on the Basics (with a tip of the hat to the Baltimore Catechism):

What does the healing?

The healing is performed by a Presence that is everywhere and out of which everything is composed, including your body.

Why does It heal me?

Because It has to if you tell It to. This Presence, Spirit, the Infinite sees what's in your consciousness and manifests around you a life experience that exactly mirrors what's in your consciousness, the good, the bad, the confused and the ignorant. The sum total of *your* consciousness has added up to a medically incurable disease. To change that experience, you must change some of the contents of your consciousness.

Change them a lot?

"A lot" is a relative term.

Why doesn't It just heal me now?

It can't. It can only reflect back at you what you give It to work with.

Why?

Because that's It's nature.

Why is that It's nature?

Read another book, okay?

I thought this was the only book I'd have to read.

Well, now you know.

Why did It let me get sick in the first place?

Let you get sick? Honey, It *made* you sick.

Why?

Because that's what It was able to do with the material It had to work with.

So, to get different results, I give It different material to work with?

Exactly.

How do I know that's true?

I suggest we argue about it for another thirty-seven pages.

No, thanks.

Oh. Well, then I guess you'll have to try it and find out.

Suppose I try it and it doesn't work?

I don't do fortunes. Now, do you want to hear this or not?

Yes, yes, I want to hear it.

Okay. You've got a terminal disease because you're in Terminal Consciousness. That doesn't mean you're a bad person or a loser or anything like that. It means that the sum total of your expectations, both conscious and unconscious, adds up to "It's time for me to get out of here." In your heart of hearts, you perceive the future as too scary, too unpleasant, too boring, as pointless, or as just plain unnecessary.

Not that I'm saying you're right, but how would I change that?

By changing the contents of your consciousness.

The opposite of death is the future.

Yes.

How do I do that? I mean, choose the future?

Choose *what* future?

Ah. I'm getting it. You want me to mentally create a future that I want to stick around for.

Yes? And do what with it?

Hm. I guess I hand it over to this Presence of yours and say, "This is what I want. Dump the disease and do this instead."

Yes. Only you don't say "do this," you say, "This is what's true about me right now."

But it isn't what's true about me right now.

The Presence only knows the present tense. If you tell It every day, "This *will* happen in the future" or "This needs to be done for me…"

Aha! It'll say, "You're right, it needs to be done for you some day. In the future." And then the future never gets here because the future is never now.

Correct. You declare every day that it's *true* until it becomes *fact*. And in between your periods of spiritual work you *act* like it's true and *plan* like it's true.

You make it sound like this Presence is a little slow on the uptake.

Oh, no. It always responds instantaneously. You and I are slow on the uptake.

Meaning, I don't have to convince the Presence, I have to convince myself.

That's right.

How will I know when I'm completely convinced and not just fooling myself?

Obvious.

Oh, right. I'll be healed.

Yes.

So, my spiritual work doesn't really need to be about my body: what's wrong with it, what needs to be fixed.

No. But surely your body will have to be part of your future.

Yeah, but I visualize a healthy body for me to live the future in. Right? I don't worry about how to get from the body I've got to the body I want.

Right. You visualize the finished product, not the process. The Infinite can work out the process.

This all sounds a little too easy. Just mentally create a future and I'll heal?

I suggest you try it before you assume that it's easy.

Imagining my future?

Not "imagining" your future. *Believing in* your future. It can't be a bullshit future. It has to be a real future. Which means:

    a) it must be a future you can actually believe in, and
    b) it must be a future that you can actually see yourself living in.

You're saying it has to be a plausible future. Plausible for me in particular.

That's right. Anybody can say, "I want to be a movie star, live in a mansion, drive a Rolls-Royce and have a blond Adonis for a lover." That's not believing in your future. That's daydreaming.

A plausible future. That's a little more challenging.

For a person in Terminal Consciousness, it's extremely challenging. Got any ideas for your future?

Now that you mention it...no.

I didn't think so. Now you've got your work cut out for you. Go to it. Have fun. It'll be great.

That's easy for you to say.

Yes, it is. Yes, it is.

2 • Do Your Daily Mental Work

Organize a daily schedule for positive imaging and stick to it. It doesn't matter what you call your spiritual work: affirmation, meditation, contemplation, spiritual mind treatment, visualizing, quiet time, prayer, whatever. Just make sure you do it every day. You're living in a world that gives you negative input every day. Make sure you're working to counteract the effects of all that stuff.

The central concept of your daily spiritual work is this: you're already well in Spirit and the disease you're experiencing is a lie; it's a fact, but it's not the Truth. You choose now to experience the perfect health that Spirit has already given to you.

Your daily spiritual work is not for the purpose of manipulating the HIV virus or controlling the symptoms of the disease. Let Spirit deal with all that. You deal with knowing the Truth about yourself. Don't fuss about how your healing will happen; that's not your job. Your job is to know that your health has already been given to you by a Greater Power.

There should be no sense of coercion in your daily spiritual work, as if you needed to force Spirit to do this for you. Spirit already has done it for you. It's your job now to know that, see it and ultimately experience it. *You're not trying to get the Infinite to do something for you, you're acknowledging a physical wholeness that is already there at the level of Spirit.*

The principal feeling in your daily spiritual work must be one of trustful surrender. You're turning the disease situation over to Spirit. You're giving it up. You're saying to the Infinite, "I certainly don't have the power to resolve this mess, but you do, so do it." Then go wash your car.

This isn't a groveling, begging kind of thing. There's no question of being refused. Spirit must respond to your believing thought; and the more confidently you announce your wellness, the more readily It will produce your healing.

It's very important that anyone who seeks a spiritual healing question his spiritual beliefs constantly. He must always be clarifying in his own mind what he thinks is true. Why does Spirit heal us? Why does It respond to our beliefs? Why would It care what happens to us? These are questions that must be answered in the course of your healing.

If your thinking about Spirit is vague, then it will make your healing that much more of an unwanted challenge. How can you believe that a spiritual Power has already granted you your healing if that Power is a complete mystery to you? It's very difficult to make demands upon a Mystery with any confidence that It will come through for you. An ongoing program of spiritual study will be tremendously helpful to anyone who seeks his healing. You need to better understand the Power which you seek to use.

Be careful not to think of your daily spiritual work as some kind of magic incantation. The words you say don't heal anything; neither do the visual images you entertain. It's your relationship with life that produces the healing. The goal of your daily spiritual work is to change your habits of thought permanently. You seek to alter the way you relate to life on a moment-by-moment basis.

That doesn't mean you have to be nicey-nicey, happy-happy all the time, or even most of the time. If that were a requirement, we'd all be dead. But it does mean you need to change your beliefs about your life. And that takes practice.

3 • Do Whatever Else Supports Your Healing

Here are some of the things that successfully healed, former PWAs have done as part of their healing projects:

Horseback riding	Paragliding
Violin lessons	Tai Chi
Gourmet cooking	Bicycle treks
Writing	Candle-making
Gardening	Painting
Software design	Furniture-making
Starting a rock band	Competitive sports
Opening a shop	Radio reading for the blind
Carpentry	Volunteer work at homeless shelters

Spiritual healing isn't about medical test results, it's about life. Your life will be just a little different than anybody else's because your consciousness is just a little different from anybody else's. Living the life you truly want to live is the goal of your healing. So, doing the things you've always wanted to do must also be part of your healing. Go do them. Show the Infinite that you mean business. And don't worry about whether or not other people understand what you're doing. Their approval isn't what heals you.

Career changes are very common in the arena of spiritual healing.* The phrase heard most often in our healing groups was, "Why don't you just do it?" Someone would say, "I've always had it in my mind to do such-and-such, but I've always been held back by this-and-that."

Why don't you just do it? was the response.

The greatest benefit of spiritual Truth—the knowledge that your life is a reflection of your consciousness and nothing else—is that you realize, finally, that there's nothing out there standing in your way. There's no such thing as an obstacle. If you want to do something, you can just go do it. The world is wide open. Nothing is resisting you.

Scary concept, isn't it?

4 • Get a New Act

The Era of the Pissy Queen is over.

With the advent of the AIDS crisis, it must be clear to anyone possessing even a smidgen of spiritual Truth that the old victim-of-the-world persona—the super-sophisticated sexual deviant slashing people to ribbons with his razor-edged tongue—is no longer viable. The Pissy Queen persona is the place where Terminal Consciousness and pathological gay cleverness come together. The savage retort, the holding of grudges, the raised eyebrow, the I'm-all-I-need-honey fake independence all combine to say, "The world sucks and

---

* Not universally so. Many people heal so that they can get back to the work they've always known and loved.

so does everybody in it. There's nothing left to do but trash everything in reach."

In response to such a consciousness, Spirit has no choice but to move the individual out of this life that he disdains so much.

Get a new act.

Over, also, is the Era of the Naughty Queen. Prancing about coquettishly, usually for the edification of straight people, in the role of the spritely Peter Pan sexual deviant capable of oh-dear-me *such* naughtiness is another junction point for Terminal Consciousness and gay cleverness. There was a time when such behavior was courageous, back when anyone could kill you for it without even getting his wrist slapped. But for a gay man of the 1990s to play the same self-demeaning role as a gay man of the 1940s is a curious kind of survival strategy.

Underlying the Naughty Queen role is the belief that to be homosexual is to be intrinsically wicked and dirty. And that is a belief that the Infinite must honor by making it the truth of your life.

Get a new act.

If we cast aside the roles of the Naughty Queen who puts himself down and the Pissy Queen who puts down everybody else, we might get around just to being people. Many gay men have already made the transition; they are often regarded as boring by the gay men who haven't.

Your new act is forgiveness.

Forgive everybody in sight. Forgive everybody you've ever known. Forgive people you've never met. Forgive the president. Forgive the Pope. Forgive Anita Bryant. The real deciding factor in affecting a spiritual healing for yourself won't be how adept you become at meditating and visualizing and affirming. Your healing will be Spirit's response to how you think in general on a daily basis. Forgiveness will keep you on the right track. It will free you from any negative crap lurking in your consciousness.

5 • Get Help

Don't try doing this sort of thing on your own. Let people help you.

The tricky part of assembling your band of helpers will be to find people who really believe you can be well. People who humor you while harboring the secret belief that you'll probably die anyway will not be much use. They're far worse than deathbed groupies because they don't look you in the eye and tell you you're going to die. They pretend to support your healing efforts while keeping their real opinion to themselves.

It would be wise to acquire some kind of spiritual counselor, if you can find one you can respect. Certainly a weekly group is desirable.

The tricky part about finding a healing group in which to participate is the same as the tricky part of assembling your band of helpers: you have to find a group that really believes you can heal. Look out for groups that state their healing goals in not-quite-straightforward ways. You're not looking for a "support" group nor do you want help in dealing with the problems posed by having AIDS. You aren't looking for "inner healing." You're looking for a group committed to the healing of the body.* And you want that group to be run by someone with real experience in spiritual healing, not just someone who's read a lot of books about healing. (You could simply read the same books to know what he knows.)

Groups that are dodgy about what they mean by "heal-ing" are usually run by well-meaning souls with little or no real experience in healing. They don't *know* you can heal, they just *hope* you can. The vague language is a safety factor, a potential exit door in case a group member dies. That's okay. They're nice guys. They want to help. But maybe they're not who you want right now.

But the bottom line is: *no help is better than fake help.*

---

* I realize that's ultimately a matter of 'inner healing,' but that's not what is usually meant by the groups who advertise themselves with that term.

You can get scared and confused on your own; you don't need assistance. You want your help network to help you stay clear and confident. To do that, *they* need to be clear and confident, especially your spiritual teacher.

At the very least, you can seek help from books. Anyone committed to daily spiritual work always refreshes himself at regular intervals throughout the day with his favorite spiritual writers. It can be hard to get inspired on some days. Get help from the writers you consider great. They're always there for you.

Lastly, be careful of that gay man's tendency to be clever. Don't turn group-hopping and help-seeking into an ongoing intellectual diversion. Just assemble whatever assistance is available to you in your environment right now and get to work.

Healing is not a hobby. Don't make it a long-term project. Get help and then get on with it.

6 • Deal With the Doctor

One of the big, hairy issues raised by people with AIDS who seek a spiritual healing is whether or not to use a doctor.

The rule of thumb, as stated above, is to do whatever you believe is in line with your healing. For most of my clients this has meant accepting medical treatment. I've known a few people who've brought about their healing by adamantly rejecting any medical interference with their bodies at all. But they're the minority, a tiny minority. Most clients have let the doctor in on their healing.

Doctors aren't "un-spiritual." Everything is Spirit acting upon Itself, and the healing power of Spirit works through doctors just as much as it works through anybody else. Medical technology is Spirit taking the form of medical technology.

The problem you'll encounter in your relationship with your doctor is the issue of authority. Who's in charge? Your doctor assumes that *he's* in charge. Of course! He's the expert.

Doctors tend to develop a weird rigidity of thought. This is appropriate in matters of medical treatment. It's their duty to be rigid. If you're under medical care, you certainly don't want your doctor to experiment on you with some wild theory. You want proven and effective treatment. But this rigidity extends into other areas of their lives. Converse casually with almost any doctor and within fifteen minutes you'll come up against some bizarre assertion about which he'll hear no argument, like, "Calvin Coolidge was our greatest president!" That's the truth, he's sure of it and you couldn't budge him with a derrick. This comes, I guess, from spending long hours every week in the role of Undisputed Authority.

When confronted with evidence of a spiritual healing, doctors almost invariably will backpedal and announce that they misdiagnosed the problem in the first place. The reasoning is, "People don't recover from this condition; you recovered; therefore, you didn't have this condition."

But in truth, you're the expert on your own health. You know how you feel. And it's you who must live with the aftereffects of the doctor's pronouncements.

The person seeking a spiritual healing must withdraw all authority from external things and other people. He must become the sole authority in his life. He must recognize that his consciousness is, exclusively, the source of his experience. As soon as he gives power to some external factor—a medical verdict, for instance—his healing is compromised.

Spiritual healing is a personal matter. It's all about your life, what you love, who you love and who loves you, your relationship with Spirit. It's not something you want your doctor to mess around with. Most doctors are more focussed on procedures than on people, and when confronted with ideas of spiritual healing, they tend to zero in on some tiny, not-very-relevant point and beat it to death.

If you go to a doctor, use his expertise as part of your healing. Don't put him in charge. He's not a good person to have in charge because, at the present stage of medical knowledge, he has no cure for you and believes that you are likely to die.

Know this: it's not your job to educate your doctor about spiritual healing. It's your job to heal.

It's not your job to win arguments with your doctor. It's your job to heal.

It's not your job to reform the medical profession. It's your job to heal.

Don't be clever. Just get well.

Doctors are used to being the final authority in all their doctor-patient relationships. When you claim that privilege for yourself, your relationship with your doctor will become...interesting. That's good. It's supposed to be interesting, isn't it?

I recently attended a small seminar centered around an "AIDS survivor" who had written a book about his experiences. After his presentation the floor was opened up for general discussion. A local AIDS activist and PWA, a very angry fellow indeed, embarked on a long, cranky harangue about the poor quality of health care in the city and the negative attitudes of the doctors. He rattled off a list of physicians who he considered to be real bastards. Every doctor he mentioned had at least one of my healing group clients as a patient. And my clients all thought these doctors were wonderful people.

It's a matter of attitude. If you believe yourself to be doomed by your disease, you'll probably dislike your doctor. After all, he's the one who gives you the bad news every month. He becomes a symbol of your problem. If you think of yourself as a protected child of Spirit, then your doctor becomes a useful, hard working person whose assistance you accept cheerfully.

Attitude also seems to affect the influence of medication. A few years ago, it was determined that the recommended dosage of AZT was far higher than it needed to be. Prescriptions were reduced across the board. One of my group members protested. He'd been taking the drug for years at full dosage, he'd never experienced any negative side effects and he was healthy as a horse. He didn't *want* to reduce his dosage.

This put him in the peculiar position of fighting for the right to continue extreme dosage of a drug that most PWAs dreaded having to take at all. When asked why he thought he'd done so well with a medicine that had produced devastating side effects in other people, he could only suggest it was because he blessed the drug every time he took it, and expressed gratitude for its good effect whenever it came to mind to do so.

———————

I attended a cocktail party and found myself in conversation with a group of people that included a prominent epidemiologist, an openly gay doctor well-known for his AIDS work. This man despised the idea of spiritual healing and had bad-mouthed me to other people rather thoroughly on more than one occasion. That night, I accepted his cold condescension towards me with a kind of resigned amusement (and a gin and tonic.) The conversation centered around AIDS and when someone asked this doctor if any of his AIDS patients were doing well, he said—clearly for my benefit—that it wasn't realistic to expect people with AIDS to "do well" because AIDS was a debilitating and ultimately fatal disease.

"In fact," he said, "I only have three patients who I'd say were doing well."

"Yeah, and I know exactly who they are," I said. I named off the three members of my healing group who used him as their doctor.

His eyes bugged out. "How did you know *that?*" he said.

Of course, I couldn't ethically tell him how I knew that; but don't you wish life had more moments like this?

Finally, know this: *if you have a medical problem, the best way to deal with it is the medical way, if a sane medical way exists.* If someone came to me with syphilis and said he wanted to heal it spiritually, I'd tell him he was being ridiculous. I'd tell him that syphilis was medically curable and that he should consult a doctor.

Perhaps it surprises you to read this. Well, don't be surprised. When I have a headache, I take aspirin. That's what I do. Spiritual healing is useful and needed when we manifest physical conditions that are beyond the reach of material medicine. It also comes into play when the side effects of a proposed medical treatment are expected to be unacceptably severe. When we contract such a condition, we are signaling ourselves to the effect that something is seriously wrong with our approach to life. Only then must we turn for help to a Power that is greater than our present circumstances and that can guide us to our healing.

7 • Don't Trade on the Disease

Don't use your medical diagnosis as a way of getting what you want out of life.

The person with AIDS who's always had trouble feeling connected to other people can find that his chronic loneliness is an obstacle to his healing. His HIV-positive status, his ARC, his full-blown AIDS can supply him with a busy social life, with something to do on different nights of the week, with a legion of helpers who'll bring him food and run errands for him, with a network of health care professionals who express great interest in his well-being and with money-for-no-work from the government, his job, his insurance policy, his relatives.

After a lifetime of loneliness, this kind of attention can be very seductive.

Don't accept it.

If you're a person seeking a spiritual healing, never allow yourself to use the disease as a way of making the world work for you. To do this is to say to the Infinite, "This disease does good things for me. It supplies me with a lot of life's pleasures. I don't want to be without it."

The spiritual seeker must accommodate the disease as little as possible. He must go to work. He must get out and play. He must shift for himself as any healthy person would to whatever extent he is able.

In the same vein, any healing group needs to have a Graduation Day for each of it's members. There needs to come a time when the client is told, "You're fine. You're well. Get out and don't come back. Go live your life." It is very inadvisable to allow a healed person to continue hanging around the group meetings every week because he can't bear to lose the social outlet. Tell him to get out.

If your healing group doesn't have Graduation Days, then promise yourself that you'll announce your own Graduation as soon as your healing is in place.

Healing may cost you some friends. You'll find that some people in your life, even people with whom you've had a long, loving association, don't like the changes they see in you. You'll be different all of a sudden. You may also ruffle the feathers of some people. They'll encourage you to get involved in AIDS-related activities, political stuff. They'll tell you it's your duty. And they won't like it if you refuse.*

8 • Don't Read Crap

The AIDS epidemic has produced a strange new breed of intellectual: the AIDS scholar. Don't be one.

Don't read stuff about AIDS: newspaper reports, magazine articles, novels, short stories, poetry. You don't have to be the world's best-informed PWA in order to heal. In fact, it would be very counterproductive to run around collecting the latest medical information on the disease. Leave it alone. You already have enough facts. Now you must reach for the

---

* My clients are often incensed at the way activists simply assume that anyone found to be HIV-positive is forever after required to offer his time as a volunteer for AIDS organizations.

Truth. Don't identify with the sick and the dying. Identify with the living.

Don't *watch* crap either. You've seen enough TV-movies about AIDS and heard enough newscasts and documentaries. Change the channel. Watch *Dallas* reruns. Watch *the Honeymooners*. Don't watch AIDS stuff. Not even if you hear it's "really good."

And don't *talk* crap. Talk about your life and where it's going. Save any talk about the disease for your healing group meetings or for private sessions with your spiritual teacher.

One of the most impressive healings I know of is a man we'll call Charles. Charles's healing was so spectacular that he was written up in one of the most prominent medical journals in the world as a "mystery remission." For a time, he was flown on a monthly basis to a major west coast AIDS research facility so that they could run tests on him. The doctors found him fascinating.

Every month Charles would sit in the waiting room at this medical center and wait for his doctor. And he began to recognize the other people in the room with him because they were there about the same time he was every thirty days. They weren't a pretty picture. Charles was the only person in the room who looked the same at every visit. The others deteriorated alarmingly.

The conversation among the PWAs in the room was all about their symptoms: I've got the thing on my foot, I've got the thing in my mouth, I've got the thing in my eye. Charles knew better than to involve himself in such talk, so he took to wearing headphones on his visits. He'd play New Age woo-woo music. Then he took it a step further and would bring metaphysical literature with him and hold the book up in front of his face. The other people in that waiting room, if any of them besides Charles are still alive, must remember him as a very strange individual indeed.

One day, someone pulled the book away from Charles' face and held up a magazine in its place. This man was very advanced in his illness, covered with KS lesions. The magazine—a major periodical you've bought copies of at some time or other—had done an article about this guy's AIDS dementia: how he forgot who he was and where he was and who everybody else was. There were photographs to go with the story. The man was sharing the article with all his "friends" in the waiting room. He was flattered. He felt honored that this magazine had written about him.

For some reason, this sent Charles off the deep end. He was enraged. He stalked into his doctor's office with the magazine crumpled in his fist.

"Why don't they write a story about *me!*" he shouted at his astonished physician. "All these people who die! Why are they all we hear about! Why doesn't somebody write an article about *me!*"

The doctor recovered himself a little, and chuckled. "Good Lord, Charles," he said. "I'd hate to think what would happen to our federal funding, not to mention our donated funding, if people heard about *you.*"

That was the last time Charles tried to talk to anyone about his healing.

9 • Eat Food

My friends who are health care workers tell me that the catastrophic weight loss suffered by many people with AIDS doesn't result from any particular wasting effect of the disease, but rather from the patient's failure to eat enough. He doesn't feel so hot, so he doesn't eat.

Food is your medicine: take your medicine. Certainly you wouldn't wait until you felt like it to take prescription medicine; you'd take it at the appointed times. Do the same with food. Whether or not you feel like eating is irrelevant. If you know it's time to take in some nourishment, then *eat.*

This raises the divisive question of what exactly you should eat, and usually generates arguments about the benefits of strict vegetarianism over octo-lacto-vegetarianism.

The correct approach to food for the spiritual seeker is simply this: eat in good consciousness. Know that all food is

Spirit in the form of food and then just eat what your consciousness knows is good for you and don't eat what it knows is bad for you.

The usual response to these instructions is to immediately classify all conventional food as poisonous and devote oneself entirely to a natural/organic diet only. If that's what's right for you, fine. However, one of my clients, during the entire duration of his healing, including a protracted hospital stay necessitated by an attack of pneumocystis pneumonia, ate the same old crap he'd always eaten: pizza, potato chips, burgers and fries. He continued to smoke cigarettes and drink vodka tonics.*

This might sound utterly suicidal, until you realize what he was up to. Eating in his usually sloppy style was his way of affirming, graphically and consciously, that he was a normal, healthy person who could eat what he liked; eating brown rice and steamed vegetables for reasons of health made him feel like an invalid.

This isn't a course of action I can recommend. But it sure worked for him.

10 • Stay Out of the Twilight Zone

People faced with a terminal illness will do desperate things to be well. And every time a new killer disease is making the rounds, there is always an exhaustive array of exotic treatments available to the sick.

AIDS has certainly generated an enormous number of exotic treatments, some based on this or that piece of western medical knowledge, some based on ancient traditions, some based on brand-new theories, all of them collected under the heading of "alternative therapies." I can't tell you which of these therapies are helpful and which are quackery. I'm not qualified to say. As has been stated above, you must do whatever you think is in line with your healing.

---

* Up to that point, I'd never known that Pizza Hut would deliver to a critical care ward. Live and learn.

Having a closed attitude towards unusual treatments is probably not a good idea, not if you're seeking a spiritual healing. Flexibility is necessary, and an open mind. On the other hand, like the lady said, "Don't be so open-minded that your brain falls out."

One thing I will tell you: in each of my healing groups there was always, at any given time, someone filling the role of Alternative Therapies Guru. I've seen about five such people come and go. These guys knew all of it. They knew where you could get the stuff you spread on bread, where you could get the stuff from France that wasn't legal in the United States, they knew where you could find a good iridologist, Chinese herbalist, Ayur-vedic doctor, aromatherapist, trance channeler or crystal healer. They knew Swami Wonchabuythis and Madame Karma von Tarot-Libra. They frequently commandeered meetings of the healing group by discoursing upon all that they knew.

All the Alternative Therapies Gurus have something in common today.

Can you guess what that is?

Go ahead and say it. It's what you're thinking.

That's right: they're all dead.

Every single one of those men who knew everything there was to know about alternative therapies eventually passed away from AIDS while other group members achieved their healings without indulging in any alternative therapies or by using only one or two of such treatments.

A person who runs around from one healing system to another has not really taken responsibility for his own healing. He has not tapped into that healing Presence within himself. He's searching around for something "out there" that will heal him, some external thing that will do the trick, some special person who knows the secret. Beware of this tendency in yourself. It indicates a lack of confidence in the healing capacities of Spirit. It is a crisis of faith disguised as a search for the Truth.

Many of my clients who have healed have used alternative therapies as part of their self-care programs. But the bulk of their expectations was always placed solidly on the "shoulders" of Spirit. So, if you feel that some exotic treatment will be helpful, don't think I'm telling you it's all nonsense. I wouldn't know.

But if you decide to use eleven different exotic treatments in the hope that one of them might work, you need to go back inside yourself and get reacquainted with the Power from which all healing proceeds.

11 • Don't Tell

While working on your spiritual healing, shut up about it. People constantly ruin their own spiritual projects by talking about them all the time. "Yes, I'm working on my spirituality, my teacher's name is Greta and she's *so* fabulous, I know I'm making progress, blah, blah, blah, blah, blah…" This is another way of trading on the disease. Your healing is a private matter between you and the Infinite. Keep it private. If you don't, you "talk all the energy out of it" and the healing probably won't happen.

Furthermore, if you're someone who's already achieved his healing, shut up about that, too. Spiritual healing isn't Alcoholics Anonymous. Now that you're healed, it's not your job to go out and teach all the PWAs in the world. Frankly, it's not a job for which you are qualified. Stay out of it. You've got your life back: go live it.

I have met and also known personally quite a number of people who achieved a healing from AIDS and subsequently decided to become a "role model" to other PWAs, to go public with their accomplishment.

All those people have one thing in common today.

Can you guess what that is?

Go ahead and say it. It's what you're thinking.

That's right: they're all dead.

Going public is usually, perhaps inevitably, a disastrous choice. The healed person who decides to make it his mission in life to heal others finds himself bombarded with negativity and disbelief from all sides from people who can't accept the idea of spiritual healing and from PWAs who are expressing the anger of the terminally ill. His able management of his own consciousness in no way qualifies him or prepares him to deal with other people's consciousness. The barrage of nay-saying can cause the healed person's faith to crumble and set him back into his old belief in disease and external power.

The desire to help others is admirable and I believe every gone-public healed person I've ever met was sincere in his desire to be of service. But there are a lot of other perks, less honorable perks, that are also attractive to the gone-public person: he is the focus of much attention, people listen reverently to his opinions (an irresistible temptation to most men,) he's a celebrity, he gets his pictures in magazines, he feels himself to be part of a community, he has a sense of purpose and, not incidentally, he stands to make some money through speaking engagements and writing.

All that is a way of trading on the disease. It's a very dangerous kind of self-indulgence. Stay away from it. If you've realized your healing, then say, "Thank you," and get on with your life. If you want to be publicly adulated, then take your newly-restored life and go out and contribute something of a public nature that will garner you the attention, the respect, the speaking engagements and the media coverage. If you want to be of service to people, there are thousands of worthy organizations in need of your time and money. If you want to make a contribution to society, then take that wonderful new consciousness you've developed and apply it to something. You are a unique expression of Spirit and you have a unique vision to express.

But if you plan to achieve your healing and then make a fortune writing about it, get a new plan. Last guy I know who tried it died within a year of publication. Stay away from AIDS. Forever. It's taken up too much of your time already. Go forward into the future and leave the disease in your past.

12 • Healing Is Not Denial

Spiritual healing isn't a matter of pretending you don't have AIDS. You do have AIDS. That's why you're doing all this work, isn't it?

At no time should you get the idea that we're saying that disease is imaginary or that physical reality is just an illusion. It's all real. We're simply saying that Spirit is ultimately what all this real stuff is made out of and that, because you are a self-aware point of consciousness, the originating Spirit responds to your beliefs. You have the ability to choose what kind of reality you want to experience. You can believe in health or illness, wealth or poverty, love or loneliness and Spirit will make it real for you.

Your illness is real and needs to be dealt with. We're not saying it isn't there. We're saying it has no business being there. We're not saying it isn't a fact. We're saying it isn't the Truth.

13 • Don't Be Superstitious

The Infinite is not some capricious dispenser of magic favors, like the Devil in the old New England legends, that waits for you to make a slip of the tongue (like asking for immortality without asking for eternal youth to go with it.)

One of the drawbacks to this new approach to spirituality is that the student can become superstitious about negativity. Every time a negative thought crosses his mind he expects a bolt of lightning to strike him dead. He cusses out a motorist who cuts him off in a crosswalk and then he thinks, "Oh, no! I was *negative!* I've ruined everything!"

Don't be absurd. If your random negativity manifested that quickly, you'd have been dead long before AIDS came along. And it seems a rather severe reaction on the part of Spirit to kill you because you snapped at a thoughtless driver. The Infinite is infinite. It's got lots of room within Itself. So, you've got a wide margin for error as you seek your healing.

14 • Don't Make a Big Deal Out of It

To have a medically incurable disease isn't Armageddon or World War III, so don't treat it as such. You've just got some work to do, that's all. Do it and be done with it. Keep it fast and simple. Accept your healing and get on with your life.

We're incessantly reminded by the world-at-large that AIDS is a big problem. And the assumption we make is that a big problem requires that we take big steps to produce a big healing.

A person with AIDS who decides to be healed often makes the mistake of gearing up for it like he was in training for the Decathlon. He sets aside a couple of years of his life to devote entirely to getting well, he makes radical changes in his personality, he participates in "spiritual" ceremonies so grandiose they look like Cher is standing in as High Priestess for an Aztec human sacrifice performed during half-time at the Rose Bowl.

Lighten up.

You're not raising Atlantis from the deeps, you're just healing. Relax, get it done, and get on with your life. Spirit is Infinite, so It can't tell a big problem from a small one. Don't complicate your healing with a lot of unnecessary qualifications and misperceptions. Healing is just healing, whether from a hangnail or from cancer.

15 • Go Meet Some People

We've discussed in earlier pages how gay men often miss out on crucial stages of their emotional development in their childhood and teen years because they must live a hetero-sexual illusion. We've discussed fake friendship, the frus-trating inability to create lasting emotional connections and the crippling defense mechanism called cleverness. We've discussed the inability to enjoy meeting new people because we fear that they will not serve our needs. And we saw "Bad Neighbor Sam" learn to connect himself to life again.

Because of this kind of emotional deprivation, many gay children grow up to be *chronically self-involved.* This doesn't mean that they are arrogant and conceited like movie stars. Quite often, a chronically self-involved person is good-natured, polite, productive, talented and fun at parties. He votes in elections, gives money to good causes and in general does no harm. But he is chronically self-involved. If he has friends it's because those friends serve him well and reinforce an image of himself that he cherishes. He is civic-minded insofar as the matter involves him directly; he is attentive to gay rights issues, but could not care less about the Rapid Transit Commission or the School Board because he drives a car and has no children. He goes to cocktail parties and political meetings not for the pleasure of interacting with people, but in order to find prospective lovers; if there is no one in attendance who he desires, he leaves.

The self-involved person is not always easy to spot. He isn't always an Event Addict or a Pump-Up-the-Muscles Strategist. He is often personable and fun to be with. He is often successful in his work (of course.) He knows how to say the right things and when to remain silent. But there is one distinct characteristic by which he reveals himself: he is inexplicably alone. He is nice looking, amusing, perhaps financially stable; perhaps he knows his way around a piano keyboard or he sings a good baritone. But he is alone. He goes on dates, but he never goes steady. He refers obliquely to past lovers in other cities, but no one seems interested in him as a marriage prospect in the here and now. What friends he has often forget to include him in their plans.

Many a gay man who seeks a spiritual healing discovers himself to be chronically self-involved. He takes up body surfing or violin lessons or he flies to the Yucatan, but none of his healing activities involve other people very much. Everyone admires his spunk, but no one seems to be making the journey with him. He hasn't made room for anyone else in his consciousness.

It is unlikely that a chronically self-involved person can induce a spiritual healing in himself, at least not one that will stick. I have seen gay men with dazzling personalities force a temporary return to health in themselves through sheer egotism; they are unwilling to appear to fail in the eyes of others. But the disease is not gone, it is only held at bay through force of will. There is something missing from their healing regimen.

The missing ingredient is: *connections.* Other people are the only legitimate reason for staying on here in this world. The connections between people are the golden cords that bind us to this life. Without them we have no anchor. We float away. If we can't let other people into our life, then we have no life. Chronically self-involved people who seek a healing usually decide to get their healing all taken care of in private and then present themselves to the world, hale and hearty, when it's all over. *Ta-da!* This is not a good strategy. Worthwhile connections with other people are a crucial factor in the healing process and should be dealt with first, not last.

This suggestion often produces extreme behavior. A person seeking his healing thinks that to overcome his chronic self-involvement means that he must become some kind of gay Mother Theresa, renouncing all his worldly goods and ministering to the poor and suffering. Next thing you know he's cleaning the bathrooms of other PWAs and serving food at soup kitchens. Certainly these are worthy activities, but we must be suspicious of the dramatic nature of his transformation. Such a change of behavior smacks of grandstanding, which is a form of cleverness, and is a symptom of chronic self-involvement. And besides, do any of these virtuous activities really serve to connect him personally with other people?

The attempt to heal chronic self-involvement can also lead to the kind of gooey sentimentalizing that we've discussed earlier. But saccharine conversations with fellow sentimentalists do not connote real friendship; they merely create the illusion of intimacy. Why is it an illusion and not the real thing? *Because you can do it with anybody.* If you want to have a gooey, sentimental conversation, all you have to do is seek out a fellow sentimentalist: any one will do. Real friendship comes with bumps and potholes. A relationship in which there is no friction, in which no incompatibilities must be confronted and worked out, is merely an acquaintance.

Most of the great, abstract metaphysical problems addressed in these pages can be healed through simple, humane behaviors backed up with spiritual clarity.

How do you heal chronic self-involvement?

Take some time.

Another symptom of the chronically self-involved person is that he detests small talk. Sitting around in the living room talking about food prices and fishing and other people's relatives makes him fidget. He wants to be talking about vast, cosmic ideas or sharing complex intellectual observations because such conversations stimulate him and expand his awareness. But baseball statistics? Children? Celebrity scandals? Who cares! It's all too boring.

Take some time.

Come down out of that abstract space where you live, and talk to some people. Talk to them about what? About nothing. It's just an excuse to be together. Talk about shoes and where to get the best burgers and what the weather was like this time last year. Don't look for any kind of profit from such talk. The profit comes from enjoying other people's presence in the room.

Put aside your busy calendar. Nothing that's on it was ever that important anyway. Even your healing activities can be set aside for this. Talk to the nice people. Make some connections.

Take some time.

After AIDS

Another too-clever question with which we distract ourselves from our real work is, "Why does the gay community have AIDS?" This is another useful delaying tactic since a) it can be debated endlessly because b) it leads us into questioning why things happen to other people. You can only know why things happen to you and, as has been stated above, not always even then.

However, if we felt compelled to come up with some answer to that question, we could, as a start, get our terms in order: for instance, even if you think the gay community is a real thing, the gay community doesn't have AIDS. A lot of gay *people* have AIDS. A lot of gay people *don't* have AIDS. It's sad that so many gay people are sick. It's not a good thing. But lots of gay people aren't sick, and that's a really good thing. If AIDS is "working its way through the gay community" and you're a member of the gay community, well, you can follow that idea through to its obvious conclusion: AIDS is working its way towards you. Are you sure you want to think about it that way?

Why things happen to communities and to other people is not your immediate concern. Why are gay people getting AIDS is not your immediate concern. Why do *you* have AIDS is your immediate concern. And if you don't have AIDS, why all the head-scratching about it anyway?

Be responsible. Take care of yourself. Treat yourself right. But for goodness sake deal with the problems that are happening, not the problems you fear might happen someday. And if you want to ponder deep metaphysical ideas, apply them to your own life, not to other people's.

If someone you love has AIDS and he's willing to do the work, he will heal. If he wants you to help him, help him. If he doesn't want you to help him, leave him alone. And if he doesn't want to heal, you can't make him.

A person's life is a matter between him and his God. We can participate in his life if he invites us in; but we can't decide to step in and interfere without his consent. Not only is that the height of arrogance, but it doesn't help; his consciousness will be his destiny no matter how much we huff and puff on his behalf, no matter how hard we work to support what we've decided are his "best interests."

One night at the healing group, one of the members lost

his temper with the others. He was tired of hearing about KS and Pneumocystis and anxiety and AIDS vigils and new treatments and the public's attitude and the president and doctors and negative friends, and on and on.

"We're supposed to be *healing!*" he snapped. "Instead we're turning AIDS into a full-time occupation! If it's your occupation, what will you do when it's gone?" He narrowed his eyes at the assembly. *"What are you going to replace AIDS with in your life?"* he asked them.

It was a good question.

Maybe you should answer it.

————————

Throughout these chapters is the unspoken assertion that humor is essential to healing. In fact, the characteristics of flexibility, open-mindedness and patience that spiritual growth requires are far easier to develop if a healthy sense of humor is in place.

Among the PWAs with whom I've worked, not even death put a damper on the tacky jokes. The group members who allowed themselves die did so in good humor. They left odd provisions in their wills, often stipulating the—very bizarre—music to be played at their memorial services. The memorial services themselves were very jolly, with the speakers cracking jokes from the podium. There was lots of laughing, sometimes to the point that the service had to stop until we could regain control of ourselves.

The laughing usually offended the relatives from Omaha who hadn't spoken to the deceased in years, but showed up for the funeral (and the reading of the will). These relatives thought our laughter was the depths of bad taste.

And who can blame them? Death is, by common definition, a catastrophe without equal, a terrible tragedy. To respond to it with anything but sadness and fear is considered to be in dreadful taste. Clearly, death is an experience that most people intend to avoid.

So, anyway, here's the tackiest death story I know:

Sorta True Story #8

The Blond Reaper

While at a seminar engagement in another city, I was invited to dinner by long-time acquaintance known to all as the Blond Reaper. Nobody ever heard from this guy unless somebody died. Not of AIDS, necessarily, just of something. If nobody we knew had died, he'd call when somebody famous died. *(Did you hear about Malcolm Forbes? Did you hear about Cary Grant?)* He was the Amazing Human Obituary Column. He, of course, claimed to have *dozens* of dear friends who'd died of AIDS.

I hadn't seen him in a long time. He took me out to dinner at one of those restaurants that have exposed brick walls and serve salads made with purple lettuce and sassafras bark.

I had known him for many years and, as people will who've known you for years, he assumed I still shared interests with him that I had in fact abandoned years before. He hadn't been around during my time of spiritual experimentation.

Throughout dinner he regaled me with tales of woe involving people we had known: breakups, spouse beatings, abortions, parent trouble, drug addiction, unemployment and, of course, AIDS. Many of the stories were about people I knew that I had known rather well, but I could no longer remember who they were or what they looked like.

Every other story was about AIDS: people broke up because one of them got AIDS, people murdered each other because they had AIDS, they fought with their parents over AIDS, lost their jobs, lost their friends, went broke, all because of AIDS. He ate voraciously, his appetite apparently stoked by his enthusiasm for his subject matter, while my appetite, frankly, faded away.

He didn't exactly understand what I did as a New Thought practitioner, that I spent all day listening to tales of breakups, spouse beatings, abortions, parent trouble, drug addiction, unemployment and, of course, AIDS—not to mention incest, murder, bankruptcy, and the contemplation of suicide. His stories could not hold the same lurid fascination for me that they held for him.

However, he was buying. So, I nodded politely and continuously.

One lengthy installment revolved around a man I had worked with in Chicago. He had gone through some bad times. He had become addicted to cocaine. He had beaten his lover. The lover had left him. The lover came back. The lover died in a terrible accident. After that, the other guy spent some time in a sanitarium. All very, very sad.

"But the worst is what happened to his mother," the Blond Reaper told me.

"Oh, yes?" I said. I could see he had saved the best for last.

"His mother got cancer," he said.

"Aha."

"But she didn't die of it."

Oh?" I said.

It seems, as the Reaper told it, that this woman was one of those remarkable cases of cancer that, for no medical reason, goes into remission completely.

I asked—as circumspectly as possible—why that was so sad.

Well, of course, that wasn't sad at all. "But," he said, "after she went to the doctor and he told her that the cancer was completely gone..."

He paused.

"Yes?" I said.

"She left the office to walk home..."

"Yes? Yes?"

"And she was crossing the street outside his office and...*she got run over by a truck!*"

He stared intently, waiting for my response.

A strange tightening occurred around the base of my throat.

"Uh, did she die?" I asked.

"Oh, yes, Greg. Killed instantly."

My lips began to quiver. My heart beat faster. Staring into the Reaper's eyes, I realized—with the same terror with which you realize that you're about to throw up in company—that I was trying not to laugh.

"Uh, let me get this straight. . ."

My stomach muscles were clutching painfully.

"She...was fine? Perfectly fine?"

He nodded gravely.

"And then...huh, huh...she went to...cross the street...ha, ha, ha, ha...and...ha, ha, HA, HA, HA, HA, HA...KABLAM!! HA HA HA HA HA HA!!!"

The Reaper's brows knit and then his eyes slowly widened until they were bugged out in horror.

"I don't *believe* you're *laughing* at that!" he said.

"But don't you see?" I gasped. "She was ...ha, ha, ha, ha...fine, and then...ha, ha, ha, ha, ha, and then,...ha, ha, ha...SPLAT!! HA HA HA HA...SORRY, HONEY, TIME TO GO! AAAAAAHAHAHAHAHAHAHAHAHA!!"

People at other tables began to stare.

"AAAAAAHA HA HA HA HA HA HA HA HAHAHAHAHAHA!!"

Fortunately we were already on coffee and dessert, so he was able to get the check and finish our evening quickly.

"AAAAAAHA HA HA HA HA HA HA HA HA HA HA HA HA HA HA HA HA HA HA HA HA HA HA HA HA HA HA HA HA HA HA!!"

I laughed all the way back to my hotel. I woke up in the middle of the night and started laughing again. I broke up a few times writing this passage.

Are you smiling?

Well, you're *terrible!*

Come to think of it, I never heard from him again.

to
Be Healed of an Illness

It's time to choose something else.

I have nothing further to learn from this disease. I set it aside as I would set aside an old overcoat.

All of Spirit is right here, right now. It contains within Itself all possibilities. All those possibilities are here right now. Any experience I desire is already here with me right now.

I choose a new experience. This is no more complicated than turning my head to look at a different view. I step out of one experience into another.

I am whole and well in Spirit right now. The experience of disease has been very real, but it is not required of me, nor is it my only option. I choose to experience health and well-being starting this instant, knowing that this wellness is already mine. This is not something I must force Spirit to do for me. It's not something I must create. It's already done. This isn't something I need to make happen. It was already happening before I chose.

How Spirit does this is not my problem. If It uses doctors or priests or eye of newt, I don't care. That's not my lookout. I simply choose, knowing that the Law is my enthusiastic servant and must bring to me that which I declare to be mine.

If other people say this isn't possible, I let them say it. I don't argue. Obviously, my new path is one they won't travel with me. That's okay. Spirit is taking care of all of us. They'll be fine and so will I.

I turn to the future. It lays before me in this world like a path of gold. It is wide open. And I'm going there. Spirit is going with me. It lifts me up, carries me forward and makes smooth the way.

Whatever problem prompted me to do this affirmation, I've forgotten it. I leave it behind me in my past and I go forward into the glory of what's happening now.

It's time to have fun.

Part Three

The Fag-Basher in the Sky

The Puritans hated bear-baiting, not because it gave pain to the bear, but because it gave pleasure to the spectators.

—*Thomas Babington Macaulay*

Many a long dispute between divines may be thus abridged: It is so. It is not so. It is so. It is not so.

—*Benjamin Franklin*

Chapter Nine

If God Is the Answer, I Want a Second Opinion

Beggars in Heaven

On the whole, human beings want to be good,
but not too good and not quite all the time.

—*George Orwell*

When I was coming out of my closet (back before the comet killed the dinosaurs), the gay liberation movement coined the phrase "Gay is Good." It sounded nice, but I almost immediately responded with, "Good for What?" After all, as Thoreau said, "Don't just be good. Be good for something."

Certainly I could see that in a free society all people should be free. I could see that homosexual activity did no harm and did not deserve persecution. But that was merely to say "Gay is okay," "Gay is socially acceptable."

But *Good?*

———

If you were a religious kid, the conflict between your moral attitudes and your sexual desires ultimately resolved itself into a conflict between your religious beliefs and your common sense, a conflict between your church-given religion and your God-given intelligence.

Many find it impossible to believe in most people's God, that cranky old man with the long, white beard sitting on a throne in outer space, looking down over the world (which He supposedly created) shaking his head gravely and saying, "Oh, this will never do!"

This God is an incompetent builder who couldn't get Creation right the first time. He had to keep wiping the slate clean and starting over, once by casting Adam and Eve out of Eden, then by flood, then by the sacrifice of His own son, and again—soon—by fire.

This God has given you desires that He regards as disgusting and has then sadistically forbidden you to express them, cursing you with disease when you do. This God is all-loving, except towards people like you, of whom He thoroughly disapproves; all-merciful, except towards people like you, whom He threatens with eternal damnation; and all-wise, except for His curious tendency to create things that He doesn't like (Satan, and war, and faggots).

This God has created a system of living that works like this: We're born into the world and make our way, often without any moral guidance whatsoever, and stumble along through loneliness, illness, frustration, and financial lack. When we seek a means of anchoring ourselves, we're confronted with a multitude of religions all claiming to be the Only True Faith. We grow older, and sicker, and dimmer, and more helpless, and more foolish, wondering all the while what the purpose of it all is, our bodies deteriorating more and more with each passing year, until we finally die, to pass on to our final reward, provided that our past conduct can stand up under the judgment of this same implacable Deity whose moral laws *have never been coherently explained to us in the first place.*

A second-grader could have devised a fairer system. Whatever the Creator is, He—It—is something far more complex, subtler, and more loving than this irritable, legalistic, fag-bashing absentee landlord in the sky who has dominated Western spiritual life for centuries.

A lot of gay people go in for alternative religions, especially Eastern religions, to escape from the Old Tyrant Upstairs and his legions of winged storm troopers. But these teachings can also be quite unsatisfying to a gay person in search of Truth. The notion of God the Mother is just as essentially inaccurate as the notion of God the Father. And all that talk about "masculine and feminine energies" can really work your gay nerves.

Heterosexual people think the whole universe is heterosexual. And many spiritual teachings assign specific gender characteristics to the different qualities and energies. Masculine means hot, hard, aggressive, dominating. Feminine means cool, passive, nurturing, supportive, and on and on. Everything that happens in the universe, these teachings tell us, is the result of two opposite qualities, masculine and feminine, interacting with each other. Which means that *absolutely everything that occurs in the whole of creation is a heterosexual union.* That's a level of arrogance for which there are no words to describe. And yet, many gay men participate in such teachings without ever questioning the essentially non-gay nature of *everything* that these teachings claim is the ultimate reality.

The belief that men and women possess opposite characteristics affects our society at every level. Certainly it affects our concept of family. If men and women are opposites that come together to make a perfect whole, then a "real" family has to have both a mother and a father in order to be complete. Our legal system is still fiercely distrustful of the idea of single parenting. Much concern is addressed to the absence of a "father figure" in a single mother household since the absence of a father allegedly deprives the children of certain essential masculine qualities in their environment, qualities which a woman can't provide because...well, she's a woman.[*]

This view of life was for a long time a major factor in the perception of homosexuality. Any imbalance in this vital

---

[*] Do we fuss equally over the absence of a "mother figure" in the single father household?

blend of masculine and feminine qualities—like a dominant mother, for instance—could turn the boys into pansies.*

The spiritual teachings that are based on assigned gender characteristics have taken a real beating in recent years now that the women's rights movement has worked up a full head of steam. Women are proving that they, too, possess the qualities of strength, forcefulness, intelligence and gallantry traditionally ascribed to men. And men are now encouraged to develop their softer qualities, to forgive, and to nurture, and to feel. The common response to this from the masculine-feminine religionists is to say, "Masculine and feminine traits can appear in either gender."

Which begs the question of why the hell you'd call them masculine or feminine in the first place.

A gay person's concept of a Greater Power needs to evolve beyond king-on-a-throne metaphors and heterosexual universes full of masculine and feminine qualities boffing each other and giving birth to little baby masculine and feminine qualities. We need a concept of an intangible, not-like-a-person God.

A sufficiently powerful telescope will afford you a view of thousands of galaxies. And in each of those galaxies are trillions of stars. And around those stars probably orbit quintillions of planets. And on one of those planets, in an insignificant quarter of a humdrum sort of galaxy, is a tiny, if intelligent, creature who is you, who believes that who he has sex with on Saturday nights can cause anguish in the colossal Intelligence that created all that universe.

That's a really gigantic kind of egotism. People have been put in padded cells for less.

Once in a while when I'm performing some mundane task—walking to the grocery store, waiting for the bus,

---

* Despite the changes in women's status over the past twenty years, the old masculine-feminine stereotypes are still firmly entrenched in the minds of even the most ardent feminists. Every straight couple I've ever counseled was grappling with those same tired old ideas of man's place and woman's place. Gay couples have the opposite problem: they're offered no traditional roles at all and must invent the structure of the relationship as they go. (This has many advantages along with the many disadvantages.)

balancing my checkbook—I'm struck, abruptly and without warning, by a powerful and exhilarating sensation of a Presence, a perception of an enfolding Intelligence that knows who I am, is devoted to my welfare totally and is keeping watch over every breath I take, over every heartbeat, over the placement of every footstep. I'm overpowered by the sense that everything is all right in my life, always will be all right and, in fact, always has been all right, even in my darkest moments.

My reaction is always one of spontaneous and over-whelming *gratitude*. I'm suddenly grateful to feel the air moving in and out of my lungs, grateful for the centuries of evolution that produced the mechanisms in my hands or legs, grateful that the sun is out, or not out, that the trees are green, or bare, grateful that I'm simply *there* doing whatever dreary thing I'm doing. My immediate sphere of attention, the mental boundary within which I feel at home, suddenly expands exponentially, taking in the building I'm in or the street I'm on, and all the people who are there with me, and the traffic beyond, and the city, and the sky.

Then, a friend waves to me from across the way, the bus arrives, the printer on my calculator breaks down and I'm back to what I was doing, but with sparks dancing in my hair.

I long ago ceased to tell anyone else about these spells of mine because

a) I know everyone else must have them and,
b) because it evokes oohs and ahs of admiration that are beside the point.

And the point is this: What I experience in these flashes is something that is always there. I don't believe I'm expe-riencing something that's been absent, a busy Deity briefly shining Its smile on me. This state of all-encompassing bliss is the unchanging environment within which each of us lives at every instant. I'm not being momentarily visited by a God that generally keeps Itself busy elsewhere.

It's I who keep myself busy elsewhere.

The message inherent in these experiences, what Spirit is saying about Itself, is clear. It says, "All of this is Me."

It sounds so simple, until you think about the implications. If everything is One Thing, if everything is an expression of Spirit, and made of Spirit, then that means *everything*, including your worst enemy, including your parents, including the Republican party, including the HIV virus, *everything*.

To adopt the spiritual outlook can really screw up your social life. It cuts down on conversation. It prevents you from taking part in a lot of victim talk, the us-against-them stuff.

I, myself, have a terrible problem because of this outlook. It gets me into all kinds of trouble with other gay people, especially the Anger Movers. Maybe you can help me with it. See: I think homophobes are beautiful.

Don't get me wrong. It's not that I think their ideas are beautiful, nor am I going to take any crap from them. But they're expressions of the same Spirit that I am, that you are. To fear them or want to hurt them would be like hating a part of myself. If everything is One Thing, and that One Thing is 100% on my side, then how can I be afraid of any part of it?

Besides, Spirit always delivers into our lives that which reflects our beliefs. If we consciously label other people as the Enemy, Spirit must invest them with the power we've assigned to them.

"To love" is simply a matter of perceiving this intangible Spirit within every part of Its creation. The great Christian divine Brother Lawrence called this "Practicing the Presence." To deliberately view each person as a perfect expression of a Perfect Mind, operating in life to the best of his or her ability, saves you a lot of arguing. To see the core of Perfection and Wholeness inside each one of us is a tremendous healing exercise.

Mothers are famous for this ability. We'll be watching a newscast about some sick man who has, say, raped a busload of nuns and then set them on fire. His tearful mother will then appear on the screen with a mike stuck in her face and cry, "He's really a good boy down deep!"

Yeah, lady, *way* deep.

But of course she's right. Within the very worst of us is a spirit of purity and strength that is never depleted or soiled by our stupidities. A mother's insistence that her monstrous child is really a "good boy" isn't a refusal to face reality. It is, on the contrary, a keen awareness of reality, of the Truth below the appearances.

Most of us talk about "liking" and "loving" as if they were different intensities of the same emotion. "We like each other now, and it may grow into love." But this is to confuse two different experiences.

"Liking" simply means that you find certain people agreeable. Their looks, behavior, interests, and attitudes strike enough of a responsive chord in you that you enjoy their company.

"Loving" is something very different. Loving is the practice of seeing through these surface particulars of person and attitude to view the untouched Being within.

The old adage says, "Love your enemies." It doesn't say, "Make everybody your friend." Clearly, it allows that we will *have* enemies. We're just supposed to love them anyway. "Love" and "Forgiveness" are the same thing.

When you're in a negative confrontation with someone, take a step backward mentally and try to see the perfect Spirit operating at the center of this stupid jerk you're fighting with. It does wonders for your blood pressure. Practice this loving technique diligently and you'll find yourself *liking* more and more people.

And remember to include yourself. Always feel free to look through your own surface appearances to the quiet Wholeness at your center. From that vantage point you can painlessly evaluate your virtues, and your nonsense.

Do Your Mindwork

Part 10: T. M. T.*

To love unreservedly and still maintain your integrity is something of a tightrope act. It's difficult also to love unreservedly the people who've caused you a lot of trouble in the past.

Relationships come back to haunt us. The people we attract into our lives reflect aspects of our thought. They reflect our opinion of ourselves. Not only do old lovers, sparring partners and other troublemakers return regularly to our lives and seek readmittance, but other people just like them appear constantly to take up their place in a pattern of experience from which we're trying to escape.

In order to have what we want, we must first reject what we don't want. As long as we continue to accept an inferior quality of experience, as long as we remain in the role of Victim of Circumstances, the Infinite can't supply us with anything better; in fact, It interprets our acceptance of bad situations as a *desire* for bad situations. Misery is a form of enthusiasm.

So, the next time an old problem-causer returns to you, or if a new person is seeking to become the latest in a matching series of problem-causers, *brand him!*

Imagine a big, glowing branding iron, like the kind they use on cattle. Use it to brand that person's forehead. It's only an imaginary branding iron, so he won't feel a thing. Brand his forehead with the letters TMT.

That stands for:

Too Much Trouble

This doesn't mean that you don't like this person. You may like them a lot. It simply represents good judgment. It

---

* This is, without any question whatsoever, the most popular technique I've ever devised. I've taught it in public only three times, once in 1989, once in 1990 and once in 1991, and yet I constantly run into people who tell me that they're using it, including people who weren't at any of those seminars.

means that as they presently are and as you presently are, nothing good can happen between you. You make each other crazy. Or in the case of a new and aspiring problem-causer, you know you *will* make each other crazy.

Every time you see this person after that, he'll continue to invite you into new and crazier situations. And as your hormones kick in, or as your greed kicks in, as you consider driving to the coast with him or attending his barbecue on Sunday, you'll see it on his forehead:

T. M. T.

"Aha, yes," you'll say to yourself. "I remember now. Too much trouble." And then you'll wisely, and cheerfully, decline his offer.

And you'll make a wonderful discovery. Once you stop agreeing to participate in their nuttiness, it's easy to love these people. You're free of all the associated negative emotion. You no longer need to control them or prove anything to them. They're these crazy people you know, that's all.

Now, they may not stick around. They may require partners-in-madness as part of their daily experience. And if you consistently decline to be such a partner, they may have to drop you entirely and go find someone more cooperative. That's okay, too.

Because once you've convinced yourself that you're fine without the kind of debilitating excitement that these people provided, that mental pattern will be shattered and the Infinite will be able to produce healthy relationships for you in response to your new outlook.

So, get out that branding iron. Use it liberally. **TMT.**

A friend of mine, a flight attendant with an unfortunate track record as regards dating, tells me that there are married men all over the east coast with TMT branded on their heads.

Sorta True Story #9

**Egon
von
Fatherworship**

Egon von Fatherworship came to me for a consultation. He told me about his life, his job, his visits to psychics, his sexual score card, his medical history, his spiritual teachers, all of which seemed to have something to do with his father.

Egon had been involved in many spiritual teachings, many of which contradicted each other (though he seemed to be unaware of any contradictions.) He assumed that I'd be very much like the other "spiritual counselors" that he'd been to see.

I asked him what I could do for him.

"Well," he said, in a voice filled with portent, "I want to see God manifest in my life."

"Uh-huh, okay," I said. "As what?"

He knitted his brows. "Um...I want to see *God manifest in my life.*"

I knitted *my* brows. I was sure he'd already said that. "Everything is God, Egon. God isn't up there waiting to come down here. All of God is anywhere. God manifests in our lives through the events and things in our lives. What do you want God to manifest as?"

He was confused. "I don't understand what you mean."

"A new car, a lover, another job? What?"

He scowled like a cardinal. After all, here was a guy who had worn strange robes, breathed incense and knelt at the feet of gurus. He'd consulted trance-channeled entities who weren't even famous. My God, he'd *been to India.* "Well, that seems rather crude, Greg," he said.

"Oh. Okay. Sorry." I scratched my head. "Let's put it this way, then: when God manifests in your life, *how will you know?*"

He thought about it. "I don't have any idea. It's never happened to me before, after all."

I sighed. He was going to make me work for my fee. Sure. Why not. "Okay, how about this? What is happening in your life right now that tells you that *God isn't there?*"

He frowned. He squinted. He drummed his fingers on the arms of his chair. This is a phenomenon often witnessed by counselors and practitioners: the client doggedly tries to avoid discussing the reason he made the appointment.

But I had him this time.

I thought.

"But Greg," he said condescendingly, "I don't want to *dwell on negatives.*"

"Oh, for crying out loud! Don't you ever just answer a question? What the hell are you doing here!"

"Okay!" he said. "Okay, okay." He sat back in his chair. He stared at the wall.

We sat quietly for a while. Then, incredibly, his eyes misted up. He heaved a shuddering sigh.

"I...have trouble getting in touch with people," he said. "I feel like there's a glass wall between me and the rest of life. Everybody seems to have a right to be here except me. I hate it. I thought it would go away. Now I'm forty-two."

We sat for a minute.

"So," I said, "you want God to manifest in your life as connectedness and a sense of belonging."

He stared at me like I'd just stepped out of a hole in the air. "Greg, that's exactly what I want."

"Okay, then. That's something God can do."

And It did.

Robbing Your Peter to Pay Paul

Whole forests are being chopped down and turned into paper
in order to print books about gays and the Bible. This is a hot
issue nowadays. Well-meaning exegetes are popping up
everywhere explaining how this or that passage in Paul or
Leviticus wasn't *really* anti-gay, or how it was merely
reflecting a hygienic or reproductive imperative of the times.

Such a waste of good trees.

Let's face it: Many of the authors of the Bible *despised*
homosexuals and said so. If you're a person who believes
that God wrote the Bible, then you must believe that God
despises homosexuals as well. Period.*

Voltaire said, "Anyone who has the power to make you
believe absurdities has the power to make you commit
injustices." The bulk of these anti-gay passages appear in the
writings of Paul of Tarsus.

"Saint" Paul.

Paul—who never met Jesus—disapproved of sex in
general, even between husband and wife, and was desperately trying to establish some kind of regularity in the sex
lives of converts who had come to Christianity out of pagan
religions that permitted all kinds of sex and that practiced
ritual orgies as a part of worship, even to the point of
maintaining sacred prostitutes in some temples.

Saint Paul was a tiresome old poop.

When he was giving advice on conduct and morality, he
was pedantic, biased, oppressive, and very boring. When he
described the workings of the Soul, however, he soared
above his dreary personal prejudices. He was a great metaphysician, even if he wasn't a very nice person.

In his highly successful campaign to organize and unite
the early Christians into a structured church, Paul embraced
a rather self-serving theology that carried Jesus's message
but wrapped it up in the vocabularies of the old religions so

---

* Any time I want to shock an audience, all I need to do is point out to them that I
am *not a Christian*. For some reason, this is considered a daring pronouncement.

as to attract converts from those faiths. As a result, many of Paul's finer spiritual writings have been grossly misinterpreted by later Christians, producing "Christian" religions whose tenets bear very little resemblance to the teachings of Jesus.

When Paul wrote his famous epistles, he was writing to people he'd taught himself or who had been taught by his representatives. So, he used terminology and made references that he knew his followers would understand perfectly without explanation; he didn't attach a glossary to his letters so that all those future generations of scholars would understand what he meant. If Paul had known that exegetes would be pouring over his little corporate memos for centuries after his death and regarding their every comma and semicolon as the Word of God, I'm sure he would have been much more careful about what he said.

We gay people have come to regard Paul as our enemy. I think that's a mistake. Certainly Paul disapproved of homosexuals—loudly, in fact.

But then, he disapproved of so many things.

If we read Paul's epistles with an open mind, we see that he used the terms "Jesus," "Christ," and "Christ Jesus" to describe *three different things.*

"Jesus" was a person. "Christ" was the Divine Mind operating through each individual. "Christ Jesus" was a way of saying that the Infinite Mind, the Christ, operated with full authority in the consciousness of Jesus. It was used to describe both the man and his teaching.

Given this explanation, listen to what Paul is telling us in his letter to the churches in Galatia:

> Now, before faith came we were confined under the [Mosaic] law, kept under restraint until faith should be revealed. So that the law was our custodian until Christ came, that we might be justified by faith. But now that faith has come, we are no longer under a custodian; for in Christ Jesus you are all sons of God: There is neither Jew nor Greek, there is neither slave nor free, there is neither male nor female; for you are all one in Christ....
>
> -Gal. 3:23-28

Christ, the Infinite Mind, God, is within each of us. Paul is telling us that Infinite Mind is no respecter of persons. Divine Intelligence works through all people with equal power, regardless of the particulars of their lives. No one— no, not even a gay person—is a pauper pleading for mercy from a disapproving God. We are each an outlet of Divine Power, able to stand eye-to-eye with any other member of our race.

Gay is good because people are good. Gay is good because you are good and I am good.

In Heaven, within us, in Spirit, there are no men or women, no gays or straights.

And there are no beggars either.

————————

So, what's left?

If you decide that Christianity is not for you and you decide that Eastern sects are not for you and New Age is not for you and New Thought is not for you and the ideas in this book are not for you and you've failed to find personal satisfaction in politics or sex or drugs or booze or culture or cleverness or intellectual pursuits, what have you got left?

You've got two things:

You've got yourself.

And you've got the silent Presence that you sense around you.

And that's all anybody's got.

The relationship you develop with that Presence will determine everything that happens to you in your life. So, what you think that Presence is will be the core question of your life.

If you think that this Presence is only the pressing weight of a material universe, you'll have a decidedly different relationship with life than if you think that the Presence is intelligent and aware. If you believe that this Presence is a grouchy, bearded emperor in the sky, you'll have a different relationship with life than if you believe It to be a Mother

Goddess in the earth. If you assign either gender to this Presence, or assign to It any kind of personality, you'll have a different relationship with life than if you believe It to be an Infinite Intelligence with no definable boundaries. If you believe that this Presence takes an active role in your daily activities, you'll have a very different relationship with life than if you believe that the Presence holds Itself aloof.

You can reach any decision you like about the nature of this Presence. It will accept any interpretation you impose on It, and It will behave like whatever you believe It to be. (This is why Spirit often seems to act like a person: because It acts through people.)

How do you find out about your relationship with this Presence? You work with It. There's no reference book in which to look up the facts, there's no one to ask. That's the catch with individuality: there's no instruction manual. How could there be? You're an individual.

You'll have to improvise. You're on your own. Or, that is to say, no one can give you your answers; they can only give you *their* answers. You're not really on your own, though. There is the Presence.

But, you may say, what about all the beautiful trappings of religion that we've always cherished? What about the Bible and Jesus, what about rosary beads and holy water, what about rote prayer, organ music, holy men and Sunday sermons and saints and angels? What about gurus and rishis and the Upanishads and mandalas and devas? What about crystals and trance-channeled entities and auras and past lives and tarot cards and chakras? What about all that?

Answer: What *about* it?

If you want special effects, go to a Spielberg movie. Your relationship with Spirit is simple. And that's a good thing, because we humans are very simple-minded creatures. We need to keep our spiritual beliefs simple or we get into all kinds of craziness.

You can find out about Spirit by talking to It about Itself.

How do you talk to It? Well, how do you talk to anybody? Just talk. If, after a while, you get no answer, then that's your answer.

But if you *do* get an answer, well...won't that be interesting?

If you must have a format, I offer this. I call it the Liar's Prayer:

Sit down in a quiet place where you absolutely can't get interrupted. Close your eyes and spend a little while imagining this hypothetical Presence. Don't overdo it. You don't want to impose characteristics on this Thing that It doesn't really possess. Perhaps you'll sense that this Presence around you is inside of you as well. That's fine, too.

Then speak to this Presence. Speak to It out loud or in your mind.

Say this:

the
Liar's Prayer

All right, you. Enough.

I give up.

Just tell me, okay?

What are you?

What are you doing here?

What do you want?

What am I?

What am I doing here?

What do I want?

What am I to you?

Am I *anything* to you?

Do you know I'm here?

Do you know who I am?

Do you like me?

Are you on my side?

Do you have plans for me?

Well, if you do, what are they?

If you don't tell me, no one else will.

So just tell me.

I insist.

I'll believe whatever you say.

Tell me right now.

Then wait for an answer...

Conclusion

There goes the good time that was had by all.
—Betty Davis remarking
on a passing starlet.

Some friends of mine and I have contemplated for some time the task of rewriting the Ten Commandments. We think it's long overdue.

Of course, debate is lively as to what the new Ten ought to be, but we have all agreed on Commandment Number One. I've been assigned to carve it on the side of Mt. Rainier here in Seattle so that people driving to work on the interstate every morning will see it. The First Commandment of the new Ten, carved in great big letters on Mt. Rainier will be:

SHUTUP

This is, after all, the first challenge to anyone who seeks the Truth about himself. We all talk too much. We all claim to know for a fact things that are really just theories. If we want to learn new truths, we must stop rehearsing what we already know.

The message of every spiritual teaching ever devised is this: *Life is not what it appears to be.* We grossly misinterpret what we see around us. We perceive as powerful things that have no power at all, and we ignore the real power that we seek, because it doesn't appear in the forms in which we expect it to appear.

The mystic's response to any assertion of fact, or any declaration of opinion, spiritual or secular, is: *Ah, but what if none of that is true?*

It's your purpose in this life to establish an intelligent working relationship with Life itself. You have within you a perfect Power that will give you everything you require if you will just take the time to get your thinking pointed in a new direction. It will heal your diseases, dissolve your loneliness, finance your goals, fill you with ideas and energy, and connect you with people and with the world, not because you've done anything in particular to deserve these things but simply because *you're there.*

The nature of this Power expresses Itself through the Law by which It works. *Thought takes form. Belief becomes experience.* Through this Law, this Presence reflects back at you what you believe. It always operates the same way through every person. It plays no favorites. It never interferes. It never says no. But because each person's consciousness is a little different, this Power often seems to treat different people with differing degrees of fairness.

This power is unimpressed by your past successes, and it is unimpeded by your past mistakes, your upbringing, or your present environment. It is not impressed by AIDS. And It certainly makes no bones about your sexual orientation.

It's my hope that the ideas in this book, entertained by a sufficient number of gay men, will help to set a new direction for the Gay Liberation Movement. We certainly need a new a direction. Up till now, the gay movement has been reactionary, a civil rights campaign given impetus by external pressures and fueled by our indignation. The AIDS crisis gave us a new external pressure to react to and the government's bland indifference to our plight gave us something new to be indignant about.

But ultimately, the future of the Gay Liberation Movement must unfold from inside each one of us. We must use the new freedoms that we've won over the past several decades. Until each of us sets about building the life he wants, we can have no clear idea of where we want to go as a group.

We can't change all gay people everywhere. We can't change the way other people behave at all. But we can, as individuals, refuse to go on being part of the problem—at all, any more, *right now.*

Some people may feel that his book has spent too much time denouncing what's false and too little time announcing what's true. Some people may feel that this book didn't devote enough pages to telling you what to think. But that's the whole point: you don't need to be told what to think. We all have different points of view, we all take different positions on the big issues, we all feel that we're at odds with each other. But at some private place within each of us, we all recognize the same truths, even if we've never heard these truths spoken. Once falsehoods are swept away by the light of reason, or simply by a little common sense, the Truth rises to the surface of the mind.

I've scrupulously avoided suggesting any "alternatives to the bars" and such like. Any attempt to do that becomes as divisive and silly as that awful ice cream social. Until we change our underlying beliefs about ourselves, almost any gathering of gay men, convened for whatever purpose, will turn into an impromptu bar scene because that's all we're able to demonstrate out of the ideas we've got.

The healing of the gay lifestyle must proceed from each individual living in it, not from some group "a-*ha!*" We've all heard the hymn, "Let There Be Peace on Earth, and Let It Begin with Me." Putting that to our own purposes, we can say, "Let There Be Gay Freedom, and Let Me Begin by Freeing Myself."

Any newer, cleaner, more open gay lifestyle will arise spontaneously from us once enough of us have accepted newer, cleaner, more open ideas about what we are and what we have a right to expect. We can never successfully impose these changes upon ourselves from the outside.

We must stop complaining and start creating. No one ever created a good life for himself by whining about how he'd been treated by mean-spirited people, or by protesting angrily that the government wasn't giving him what he needed. Creativity proceeds from within. It doesn't depend on external factors for its success.

What must we create? You tell me. That's your lookout.

All I can tell you is that we must stop trying to create as a group. Each of us must create his own life. For years, we've been trying to do it the other way around: we've tried to create groups, and a community, that would foster our personal growth as individuals. It hasn't worked. To change the world, we must begin at the personal level and see what develops; maybe a community, but maybe something else.

To see to your own creative needs, and to get in touch with your own desires doesn't cut you off from daily life. It doesn't make you self-involved and useless. It doesn't turn you into a "me-first" kind of person.

On the contrary, it gives you something to contribute.

We gay people have invented a group identity for ourselves while under fire from a society that disapproves of what we are. And we've created our identity by observing the society around us instead of by observing ourselves. As a result, we've become who we thought we needed to be instead of who we can be.

We all stand now on a platform of ideas that we believe are true, ideas about homophobia, politics, relationships, health, the future and, of course, oppression, oppression, oppression, oppression, oppression. On this platform we relate to each other. From this platform we address the straight world and announce our demands. But it seems that at no time do we do what the spiritual seeker must do if he intends to grow in his awareness: we never step down off that platform of assumptions, stare at it bravely and say: *Ah, but what if none of that is true?*

This isn't to say that all of it really is untrue. We might find that many of our assumptions are correct. But what if we decide they're not true? Suppose the basic premise of every spiritual teaching is correct, and life is not what it appears to be? *What if none of that is true?* And if none of that is true, then what *is* true?

What *is* true?

What *is* true?

Envoi

Many shall come in the name of Truth and say, do this, or do that—music, dancing, all sorts of amusements. But Truth says beware, be not deceived, seek first the truth, and all the above will be a pleasure to you.

This is a trying scene to go through; it seems as though you must leave all the world's pleasure, and seclude yourself from society. But this is not the case; you will like society all the better.

—Phineas Parkhurst Quimby
(1802-1866)
originator of
Scientific Spiritual Healing

A (Very) Brief History of the New Thought Movement

The New Thought movement began—or, at least, became something you could identify as a movement—with a New England clock maker and inventor named Phineas Parkhurst Quimby who stepped forward publicly in the 1840s. But the philosophy upon which the movement was based had much earlier beginnings.

In the 18th Century, the European philosophers began to question everything that their world took for granted—including the necessity of government by monarchy—and sought to cast doubt on all the theological assertions of the entrenched religions. This philosophical school was represented in France by people like Voltaire, Diderot and Rousseau.

In the turbulent American colonies this rational approach to life and spirituality came to be known as *Deism.* It was a new way of thinking about God and humanity's relationship to God. It perceived Spirit as an infinite Presence without human form (though they often referred to It as "He") and believed that It was kindly disposed towards everyone, no matter their religion, color or country of origin. They believed also that Spirit communicated directly with each individual within his or her own mind, without the intercession of priests and other such dignitaries. Deism was the source of the then-radical concepts of "life, liberty and the pursuit of happiness" that were expressed in the Declaration of Independence. (Please note: the American Founding Fathers—Franklin, Jefferson, Washington—were not Christians and would be disturbed to hear themselves referred to as such. They were Deists. Neither was it their intention that America be a Christian country, a situation that must have them spinning in their graves today.) The philosophy was subsequently known as Transcendentalism in the 19th Century and boasted the likes of Ralph Waldo Emerson and Henry David Thoreau.

In the 1830s, Park Quimby was diagnosed with tuberculosis, the "AIDS" of his day. His inquisitive inventor's mind refused to accept the terminal diagnosis and he embarked on a series of curative experiments, some of which seem rather comical to our modern perspective (deep breathing on horseback, for instance).

They worked. Quimby was healed of the disease. But when he put other tubercular people through his strange health regimen, they were *not* healed. This left Quimby with an interesting riddle: if it wasn't his odd healing practices that cured him, then what did? Because, if there was one thing he knew for a fact, it was that he no longer had tuberculosis.

He theorized that perhaps he was healed because he *believed* he would be. And his investigations into that hypothesis produced the spiritual system, still in use today, of healing medically incurable disease by healing the consciousness of the one afflicted so that the power of the Infinite can heal the body. *This was the first time that this Deist concept of Spirit had been scientifically applied with a repeatable technique for the purpose of producing material results.*

Quimby has been almost entirely forgotten, but in his own day he was a celebrity because of the healings he was able to produce and he taught informal classes in what today we would call New Thought spirituality. One of his more striking achievements was the healing of a very sickly Boston lady named Mary Patterson. There still exists today an eyewitness description of Mrs. Patterson being carried upstairs in a chair for her first meeting with Quimby because she was too ill to walk. Mrs. Patterson, once healed, became an ardent student of Quimby. Newspaper articles have survived written by her in praise of him, as well as other manuscripts written in her own hand that credit Quimby with the discovery of this healing system. She later began her own teaching career and, having divorced Mr. Patterson and married Mr. Eddy, she appeared before the public as Mary Baker Eddy, the founder of the Church of Christ Scientist.

After Quimby's death, things got a little strange: Mrs. Eddy began to disclaim any association with Quimby, saying that he was just a second-rate hypnotist that she had once contacted briefly. She claimed that everything she knew about healing came to her by way of Divine Inspiration. There is no way for us to know why she did this, but it set in motion a decades-long controversy and created a break between Christian Scientists and New Thought advocates that is still in place today. When Quimby's papers were finally put into print in 1922, the controversy died; the notes contained the aforementioned manuscripts and newspaper articles by Mrs. Eddy and a copy of Quimby's class notes which appear in revised form as a chapter in Mrs. Eddy's famous book, *Science and Health with a Key to the Scriptures.* The Quimby-Eddy debate is not a welcome subject with Christian Scientists today—many have never heard of it—and is regarded as irrelevant in the New Thought teachings. Most Christian Scientists who know what New Thought is see little connection between it and their religion and New Thought proponents regard Christian Science as a very distant cousin of New Thought. The two teachings have a little in common, but many differences; one example, of considerable importance, is that New Thought has no objection to the use of doctors.

However, had Mrs. Eddy not been such a difficult individual, there might never have been a New Thought movement. Many people of remarkable spiritual clarity did not wish to serve in an auxiliary capacity to her and so broke away and started their own organizations. (New Thought teachers on the whole have, shall we say, big personalities.) One of these was Emma Curtis Hopkins. Mrs. Hopkins (the existence of *Mister* Hopkins is and always was in doubt) was a student of Mrs. Eddy's. She and Mrs. Eddy had a falling out and Mrs. Hopkins went off to start her own group. Mrs. Eddy forever after referred to Mrs. Hopkins as "the Mind Quack."

Mrs. Hopkins was also quite famous in her day and late in her life became the teacher of young Ernest Holmes, author of *the Science of Mind* (and many other books) who went on to become the leading New Thought teacher of the Twentieth Century. Holmes throughout his career praised Mrs. Hopkins as the teacher who finally enabled him to get past the academic understanding of religions and philosophies and into a powerful and abiding experience of Spirit Itself. Holmes taught thousands of people, many of whom in turn became teachers and created an enormously successful New Thought movement for the 20th Century.

The largest New Thought organizations active today are both churches (a situation that would have infuriated Quimby, who disdainfully referred to all organized religion as "priestcraft"). They are the United Church of Religious Science and Religious Science International, both of which have multinational networks of member churches and societies. However, there are many other smaller organizations around the world that refuse to use the "church" appellation or any trappings of traditional religion.

Just as Christian Science and Religious Science are often casually assumed to be the same thing because the names are similar, the New Thought movement and the New Age movement are also often lumped together because they sound alike. But New Thought has several basic tenets that put it at odds with New Age in crucial ways:

First, New Thought teaches that the Infinite speaks to each individual directly within the privacy of his or her own consciousness and that all of Spirit's wisdom is available within the individual's mind at every moment; this precludes the use of sacred texts, fortune tellers, trance channellers, UFO pilots or any other external source of spiritual authority. Second, New Thought teaches that the power of the Infinite can be triggered solely by the individual's thought without the intervention of any outside support; this eliminates the use of magic objects, talismans, crystals, pyramids, spells, supernatural allies or any other external factor.

However, the basis of New Thought is to make the student spiritually independent, so the parent organizations interfere very little with the work of their member groups. As a result, New Thought is taught in a wide variety of formats: some teach it in the old, hard-line New England manner, but others teach it as a New Age practice, some teach it as a form of Eastern mysticism and many others teach it as a kind of modernized Christianity. A person who prefers one approach over another might have to shop around before he finds a New Thought group that supports his personal growth. And shopping around can be frustrating; there is a great concentration of New Thought organizations in southern California, but they are spread rather thinly everywhere else.

However, New Thought is principally a personal discipline, and ultimately the student is responsible for his own progress. This emphasis on individual effort and achievement is probably why New Thought never has and never will generate a powerful, centralized, missionary-type institution with a uniform approach to Truth; the students wouldn't stand for it.

Suggested Reading

Easy

Frederick Bailes, *Hidden Power for Human Problems*
Raymond Charles Barker, *The Science of Successful Living*
Emmet Fox, *The Mental Equivalent*
Thaddeus Golas, *A Lazy Man's Guide to Enlightenment*
Gerald Jampolsky, *Love Is Letting Go of Fear*

Less Easy

Horatio Dresser, ed., *The Quimby Manuscripts*
Ernest Holmes, *How to Use the Science of Mind*
Ernest Holmes, *This Thing Called You*

Brilliant, but slow going

Ralph Waldo Emerson, *Essays, 1st and 2nd Series* (1841, 1842)
Thomas Troward, *The Edinburgh Lectures* (1909)